SHE

Please return / renew by date shown.
You can renew at: **norlink.norfolk.gov.uk**
or by telephone: **0344 800 8006**
Please have your library card & PIN ready.

8/6/13

D1494440

About the Author

Growing up on the edge of Snowdonia National Park, in North Wales, Phoebe Smith was bitten by the outdoor bug. Her love of dramatic landscapes has since led to walking and backpacking adventures all over the world – from wild camping on the Scottish islands to sleeping under a swag in the Australian outback and watching the Northern Lights from a wigwam above the Arctic Circle. She has enjoyed snowshoeing in the Swiss Alps, scrambling in Wadi Rum and canyon walking in the US. Of all the places she has been, however, it is the UK (in particular the coastal areas) that holds a special place in her heart.

Phoebe is currently editor of *Wanderlust* travel magazine. She has also written for *Trail, Country Walking, The Guardian, Backpacker* (USA), *Lonely Planet* and *Australia and New Zealand Magazine*, and is the author of *Extreme Sleeps: Adventures of a Wild Camper* and *The Camper's Friend*. When not planning her next escapade, she is most likely found in the mountains, powered by nothing more than her own feet.

THE PEDDARS WAY AND NORFOLK COAST PATH

by Phoebe Smith

2 POLICE SQUARE, MILNTHORPE, CUMBRIA LA7 7PY
www.cicerone.co.uk

© Phoebe Smith 2013
978 1 85284 707 4

Printed by KHL Printing, Singapore.

A catalogue record for this book is available from the British Library.
All photographs © Phoebe Smith and Neil S Price.

Dedication

For my Mum and Dad who were there when I took my first steps on a much longer journey…

Acknowledgements

With thanks to Neil without whom some of these amazing photos would never have appeared.

Advice to Readers

While every effort is made by our authors to ensure the accuracy of guide-books as they go to print, changes can occur during the lifetime of an edition. If we know of any, there will be an Updates tab on this book's page on the Cicerone website (www.cicerone.co.uk), so please check before planning your trip. We also advise that you check information about such things as transport, accommodation and shops locally. Even rights of way can be altered over time. We are always grateful for information about any discrepancies between a guidebook and the facts on the ground, sent by email to info@cicerone.co.uk or by post to Cicerone, 2 Police Square, Milnthorpe LA7 7PY, United Kingdom.

Front cover: Sunset walking below Hunstanton's famous striped cliffs

CONTENTS

Footprints are soon swallowed up by the sea, as are parts of the Norfolk Coast Path between Cley next the Sea and Weybourne (Stage 8)

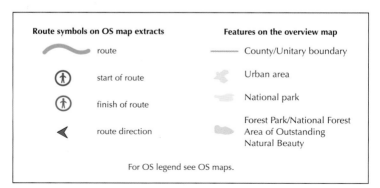

Route symbols on OS map extracts

~~~~~ route

🚶 start of route

🚶 finish of route

◄ route direction

Features on the overview map

—————— County/Unitary boundary

Urban area

National park

Forest Park/National Forest
Area of Outstanding
Natural Beauty

For OS legend see OS maps.

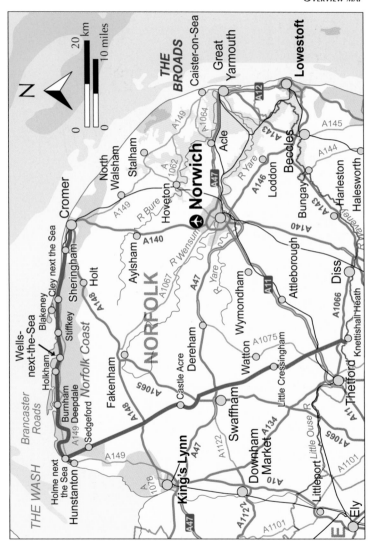

Crab baskets and boats in the fishermen's yard at Brancaster Staithe (Stage 5)

INTRODUCTION

The Norfolk Coast Path encounters cliffs at Weybourne (Stage 8)

Wilderness is something so many of us search for on our small island. Many will tell you that – if anywhere – it can be found in the mountainous hinterland of the Highlands; others will argue that, if you know where to look, it can be discovered within the southern extremities of Snowdonia. Few, if any, will try to convince you that it can reside here, in East Anglia. But it does.

The landscape through which the old Peddars Way and Norfolk Coast Path cleaves its very determined way is very special. Stand on Blakeney Point or on the edge of the beach at Holkham, or even the dunes of Holme next the Sea in the bracing wind, and you will feel how wild this stretch of coastline can truly be. And it's not just the landscape that can evoke the feeling of unbridled wilderness. Despite an ever-growing population, this region is still one of the most unpopulated in the country. Take a break in the Breckland woods just minutes from the start of the route and you'll experience just how quiet, and how still, this eastern corner of Britain can be. Better yet, visit in the winter when the wind carries a frosting of snow that cakes the golden sand dunes in crisp white powder and ices the hedgerows with a dazzling coat of rime.

The significance of the route is borne out by its long history since the

9

the invading Romans set the native Iceni (whose ancestors had used it long before their captors arrived) the task of constructing part of it in AD61 under the gaze of ancient Bronze Age tumuli. Indeed, even before then, people had lived under the big skies amid the saltmarshes, cliffs and sandy beaches for many millennia.

A combination of two separately designated paths, this 155km (96-mile) National Trail could certainly, above all others in the UK's network, be described as a walk of two halves. But that applies to more than just its physical demarcations. The route passes through remote landscapes as well as villages and seaside resorts, and can be as busy as it is peaceful, as wild as it is tame. Step into Hunstanton after treading the fields

near Fring and Sedgeford and you'll feel as though you've entered a different world. Enjoy convenient fish and chips and a cup of tea in Sheringham after negotiating the crashing waves and falling shingle at Weybourne while spotting migrating birds swooping overhead, and you will have had two mirror-opposite experiences within a period of hours.

On the Peddars Way, Roman roads make way for more modern tarmac affairs until you're plunged back into walkways lined with Scots pine. Picture-perfect chocolate-box villages lead you to vast clay fields smattered with lumps of white-coated flint and pockmarked with marl pits from our ancient farming past. Bronze Age tumuli and earthworks sit alongside 11th-century castle ruins as modern

Cromer Pier is a fitting end point to the walk (Stage 8)

sculptures echo words from the past until, finally, you reach the sea.

Once at the coast Victorian resorts – complete with all the trimmings of striped deckchairs, chippies, donkeys and amusement arcades – vie for attention then, just as suddenly, peter out as the striped cliffs descend to the waves and rare birds swoop and dive overhead. Stunning untamed salt-marshes attempt to lure you from the path as you make your way past open vistas of sparkling sand. Further along the route come wooden beach huts and family parties, followed by crumbling military remains from World War II and the wide open expanses of farmland dotted with de-sailed windmills, before a glorious finale at the pier in Cromer.

The true beauty of this walk lies in the variety of landscapes, architecture, history, wildlife, people and emotions encountered en route – a real rollercoaster ride from start to finish, which draws people back time and again.

GEOLOGY

Norfolk has a varied geological history spanning some 140 million years. Clay, sand, carstone (sandstone), chalk, flint and limestone are all encountered as the path traverses a landscape that was scoured and carved by a series of advancing and retreating glaciers during the last Ice Age.

The melting of the glaciers and subsequent reduction of pressure on the land mass resulted in a significant fall in sea level over 62 million years ago, leaving the area that is now Norfolk as dry land. More recently (two million years ago) incoming shallow seas deposited sediment – one of which is the Cromer Forest Bed Plantation (see Stage 8).

Another period of Anglian glaciation (going back 450,000 years) eroded the land to form boulder clay and gravel ridges (in Cromer and south of Blakeney), the mix of which, along with sand, created the Brecks. This unique gorse-covered sandy heath, covering $1015km^2$, is traversed on parts of the early stages of the Peddars Way in north Suffolk and south Norfolk. After this glaciation and erosion a series of hot and then cold phases caused the ice sheets covering the whole of Norfolk to melt, triggering a rising sea level, which began filling what we know as The Wash. This significant coastal indentation between Skegness and Hunstanton is instantly identifiable on any map of the UK.

Today the continually changing tides still shape the land, creating a coastline that is a combination of salt-marsh, sand dunes, chalk cliffs and gravel ridges. Further geological discoveries are being made all the time, from the unearthing of sabre tooth tiger remains in the Cromer Forest Beds, to the West Runton elephant (twice the weight of an African one) found in December 1990 and thought to have lived 600–700,000 years ago.

The church and war memorial at Ringstead is passed on the Peddars Way (Stage 4)

This landscape has a fascinating story to tell.

For more information see www.naturalengland.org.uk and click on Geology.

HISTORY OF NORFOLK

When walking some stretches of the National Trail you won't see another person for miles, yet on others – especially in summer when passing through the coastal resorts – you won't believe how many people there are. But one distinctive feature of the entire route is that there are, throughout its length, parts that feel barely touched by the hand of man. So it comes as a surprise to learn that this area of Norfolk has been populated for hundreds of thousands of years.

Archaeological finds along the coast and further inland, where scores of tools, coins and the oldest example of a hand axe have been discovered, are proof of human habitation since at least the last Ice Age, around 700,000BC.

From small beginnings, when tiny communities populated its landscapes, the area that is now Norfolk became a hub for production with the arrival of the Bronze Age (around 2000BC). The coast was clearly important for work and also for spiritual practices; a wooden type of altar named Seahenge has been found at Holme next the Sea, dating from 2050BC. There are also many Bronze Age tumuli (burial mounds) on the inland section of the National Trail.

During the Iron Age (from 800BC) the population of the area increased, but its most famous residents came in 1BC with the arrival of the Iceni tribe. These people settled, and built roads – possibly including the Peddars Way in its earliest form – houses, towns and even forts. They were not strong enough, however, to keep out the Romans in AD43, who had already dominated many other native peoples. The Romans began building their own settlements, replacing the Iceni forts – among them Branodunum in Brancaster (Stage 5) – and forcing the local people to construct new roads, including the one that would become the Peddars Way. There was a minor rebellion in AD47 so it was agreed that the now infamous Boudicca's husband could rule independently as a 'client king' in what is now Norfolk.

All was peaceful until his death in AD61. Under Iceni law Boudicca would have succeeded her husband, but under Roman law only a male heir could take charge and she was denied her right, flogged by the Romans and her two daughters raped. Understandably she went on to lead the mass uprising again the Romans which nearly toppled their British colony. Ultimately, however, she was unsuccessful, and the Romans continued to rule here until the end of the occupation in AD410.

Slowly the evidence of their domination began to disappear and the arrival of new tribes from north-west Europe marked the start of the new Anglo Saxon culture in Britain. Many remaining Roman relics were destroyed. At that point the area became part of the Kingdom of East Anglia and new towns were built.

Around AD865 the kingdom was threatened once more when the Vikings attacked, and in AD869 the king – Edmund (later martyred and commemorated in a chapel, the remains of which sit on the coast in Hunstanton – Stage 4) – was killed.

The Vikings then ruled for over 200 years until the Norman Conquest in 1066. By the 14th century farming had became the main activity in the now prospering county. Crops were grown, peat extracted and animals raised. Castles and churches were of great importance in the country at this time and Norfolk had more than its fair share, with key examples of both found in Castle Acre (Stage 2).

In the 19th century the decline in agriculture meant that many wealthy landowners were forced to sell their estates, but with the rise of the British seaside resort in Victorian times it was now holidaymakers who began to invade. During World Wars I and II the landscape of coast and country changed once again with the arrival of the military (see Stage 1, 'Military presence on the Peddars Way'). Villagers were forced to leave their homes – and in some cases never return – so that the army could train. The coast was patrolled and defences set up, some of which still remain today.

Nowadays the landscape through which the Peddars Way and Norfolk Coast Path pass has telltale signs of the past. Whether Bronze Age tumuli, the traces of Roman forts, military gun cupolas – or, indeed, the very track underfoot – when walking the National Trail you become just another one of the many people who have trodden the ground over the years. It is somehow comforting to know that, in years to come, many more will follow in your footsteps.

HISTORY OF THE TRAIL

Officially the Peddars Way and Norfolk Coast Path was opened as a National Trail in 1986 at a ceremony presided over by the Prince of Wales at Holme next the Sea. Before that both trails existed as separate entities, the Peddars Way taking in the Brecks and farmland of Norfolk, and the coast path taking walkers on a meander along the cliffs and shingle on the edge of the North Sea. Back in the 1960s the Peddars Way was considered for Long-Distance Path (now National Trail) status as one of several old trackways to be preserved. However it was thought that its 79km (49 miles) were not sufficient and so it was eventually decided to link it with the coast path (itself a combination of existing paths and rights of way, along with newly negotiated thoroughfares) to create the 155km (96-mile) route as it stands today.

The war memorial in Hunstanton marks the end of Stage 4

Although marked on the OS map as a Roman road – and it certainly shows characteristics of one, being die straight – and built around AD61 to link the stronghold of Colchester with central East Anglia, the Peddars Way is believed to have been constructed over a more ancient track. Its name is not Roman in origin and may have originated in the 16th century, merely as a generic name for a walkway. Even after the demise of Roman occupation and military use it remained in place, used by travellers and drovers, thanks to its sturdy construction and ease of navigation.

As well as being a National Trail in its own right, part of it forms a section of the Ridgeway, which includes the Wessex Ridgeway and the Icknield Way.

Trail length

A quick search online will reveal that when it comes to the Peddars Way and Norfolk Coast Path National Trail distances given range from 90 to 96 miles, and 150 to 156km. This discrepancy is due to two main factors. The first is simple: the official figure is only given in miles, so those wanting to use the more OS-map-friendly kilometre need to convert the figures, resulting in variations due to rounding.

The other reason is that the two official path distances added together (49 miles for the Peddars Way, and 47 miles for the Norfolk Coast Path) give a total of 96 miles. This is the

If you want to show off your walking credentials you can bag yourself the official badge from the National Trail management team (see Appendix B)

'true' distance, but some people do not bother heading to Hunstanton from Holme next the Sea (to avoid the there-and-back) which gives a lower distance. So there is no 'right' distance – it all depends what you're doing, and ultimately it makes no difference: it's still a great walk. For the sake of clarity the route distance described in this book includes the there-and-back to Hunstanton. Note too that all distances are rounded up to the nearest 0.25km.

WILDLIFE

Those walkers who like to indulge in a bit of wildlife spotting will find much to enjoy. Mammals, insects, birds and reptiles are all regularly seen on this particular National Trail.

Bird lovers will be in their element as this is one of the best places in the UK to see a range of waders and seabird species, as well as visiting migrants. In addition to spotting birds en route, there are several special birdwatching reserves encountered along the way. Look out for fulmars on the Hunstanton cliffs (similar in appearance to seagulls), avocets, terns and geese in the inland waterways and marsh harriers in the reeds along the seafront. On the coastal section keep your eyes peeled for bittern, skylark and lapwing, particularly at Cley Marshes, Holkham and Holme Dunes.

On the Peddars Way you might spot bullfinches, sparrows in the woodland sections and yellowhammer, songthrush, nightjar and linnet in the Brecks and in scrub, gorse and hedgerows. Also look out for muntjac and Chinese water deer, which have a tendency to dart among the trees in the forested sections. More common, but just as exciting to witness, are badger, hedgehog, hare, mink, fox, weasel, water vole and, at night – with luck – the pipistrelle bat.

On all stages of the path you might see some reptiles, such as common toad or frog, the more unusual natterjack toad and great crested newt, or the more elusive adder.

PLANTS AND FLOWERS

There is an abundance of stunning native and non-native species to look out for along the route, from the more familiar bluebell, common poppy,

Snowdrops line the early stages of the Peddars Way

snowdrops and cowslips to the best avoided giant hogweed and the more exotic-sounding Himalayan balsam, sea holly, water mint, yellow-horned poppy and meadow saxifrage. It is always worth keeping an eye open, no matter what time of year you are on the trail. Here's how to recognise a few noteworthy varieties.

Giant hogweed An imposing foreign species, recognised by its dark green jagged leaves that end in a spike, and clusters of small white flowers. This plant is not just imposing to look at; at around 5m high it hinders the growth of adjacent plants, and it is an offence (Wildlife and Countryside Act 1981) to plant or encourage one to grow in the wild. Walkers need to be careful because it is toxic; the leaves and stems are covered with tiny hairs that harbour a poisonous sap. Just a quick brush past, and you will soon know about it. The sap causes skin to become photosensitive so that exposure to sunlight leads to severe burns and blisters.

Himalayan balsam First introduced into the UK in Victorian times as an ornamental garden plant, this purple/pink-flowering species went 'feral' and is now the tallest annual plant in the country. Its height and dense growth not only prevents native neighbouring plants from getting sunlight, but its prolific nectar production draws pollinating insects away from other plants too. As it dies away in the winter its growing areas – normally riverbanks – are left bare. Stringent measures are taken to try to control it. It is recognised by its shiny spear-shaped dark green leaves, with red ribs and red-pink stems.

Meadow saxifrage Keep an eye out for this rare species on the sections of the National Trail that pass through grassy meadows and churchyards, or run along roadside verges. Now in decline as a result of changes in landscape use it is often found in groups and is has distinctive five-petalled white flowers, long stems and kidney-shaped leaves. It is easiest to spot in the spring.

Sea holly This plant is definitely one to spot on the Norfolk Coast Path. Identified by its white-edged, green-blue spiked leaves and blue flowers, it tends to grow around the sand dunes, making it particularly vulnerable due to damage from human activity. Up until the 20th century the roots were used as a sweetmeat, and the Elizabethans believed it to have aphrodisiac qualities. The best time to see sea holly is summer and early autumn, particularly around Wells-next-the-Sea.

Water mint Whenever the leaves of this plant are crushed – usually underfoot – they release a fresh and minty scent. You will see – or rather smell – this species in the wetter areas of the county, around ponds and river edges. Look for a cluster of blue/light purple-coloured flowers.

Yellow horned-poppy Boasting the largest seedpod of any plant in Britain, this species is found on shingle banks and beaches in summertime. Identify it by its bright yellow four-petalled flowers and big waxy leaves, coated with small hairs.

Viper's bugloss Walking through Breckland on the first stage of the Peddars Way, in summer, you might be lucky enough to spot swathes of these bright blue, trumpet-headed flowers. Although its habitat is mainly inland, it can also be found growing on sand dunes and shingle.

Hound's tongue Its name not only gives an indication as to what it looks like – long leaves with a greyish tone (like a 'hound's tongue') – but it was also, at one time, used as a treatment for dog bite. Its deep red flowers will be on show in springtime. Look out for it in Breckland, and occasionally on the coast near Blakeney Point.

ART

The big skies, rugged coastline and twisted trees of the Breckland that span the length of the Peddars Way and Norfolk Coast Path have, unsurprisingly, inspired many authors and artists to write, draw, paint, sculpt, and take photographs. Along the route a large number of artist's workshops and photographer's studios are passed, each of which offers a unique perspective on the beauty and wild nature of the area.

The Songlines stones

Dotted along the Peddars Way are five Norfolk Songlines stones created by sculptor Tom Perkins as part of a project with storyteller Hugh Lupton, singer Helen Chadwick and artist Liz McGowan. It is based on the Aboriginal Australian belief of songlines, where ancient tracks are said to tell stories within a much bigger 'song' about how the landscape came to exist. It makes sense when you think about it; the Peddars Way's pre- and post-Roman origins gave the path its straight line. Subsequently rights of way and boundary factors introduced more manmade curves, changing its character. A lot can be learned about man's past by looking at a simple pathway.

As Hugh Lupton, very aptly, puts it: 'As you walk the Peddars Way you find yourself becoming more and more aware of all the others who have trodden the same ground, whether they be Stone Age hunters, Roman soldiers, Saxon settlers or Medieval pilgrims. But remember that you, walking in your time, are as much a part of everything that surrounds you as any other traveller has been. All the past that has led to your moment in time is held like a great secret in the landscape that surrounds you.'

For more details about the project check out www.norfolksongline. co.uk.

WHAT TO TAKE

Unless you are camping – when a tent, sleeping mat and bag and possibly cooking stove and gas is required – a standard daypack should suffice for this long-distance path. The following list is not exhaustive, just kit suggestions to make your walking more comfortable.

- Rucksack (approx 30 litres)
- Dry bags (rain is always a possibility; useful for organising pack contents)
- Water bottle/hydration bladder
- Waterproof jacket
- Waterproof trousers
- Walking trousers/shorts (water resistant, durable fabric, articulated knees)
- Base-layer top (not cotton; go for wicking fabric to keep you cool and dry, either synthetic or merino wool)
- Fleece/softshell jacket (warm midlayer to wear over base layer and under waterproof jacket)

- Walking socks and spare pair (flat-locked seams to prevent rubbing)
- Walking boots/approach shoes (whichever are more comfortable)
- Hat (woolly in winter, sunhat in summer)
- Gloves
- Buff (to keep the wind off your neck; can also be used as headband/hat)
- First aid kit (don't forget the blister plasters and painkillers)
- Food (slow-release energy snacks such as cereal bars, dried fruit and nuts)
- Maps and compass

Look out for the acorn symbols that mark the National Trail

WAYMARKING, ACCESS AND MAPS

As with most of the National Trails in the UK network, for the most part waymarking is good. Some sections – especially on the Peddars Way – are not always clear as signs have been vandalised or are obscured by undergrowth, but looking at the map and having a brief exploration of the area will help you find the correct route without any real problems. Following the Norfolk Coast Path is a breeze – as long as you keep the sea to your left as you head from Hunstanton to Cromer, you cannot go wrong!

Access-wise the route is on well-established paths and bridleways so a complete walk can be undertaken on most occasions with no issues. The military area passed on Stage 1 is out of bounds to walkers and, as there are many signs advising of the danger and fences erected to enclose the area, there is no way you can walk off-path inadvertently. Heed the warnings and stick to the designated track.

There are no huge sections of ascent or particularly difficult terrain. Most of the walk is on forest tracks, country lanes, sand, waterside paths and along cliffs, with a few sections of shingle.

Along the coast the two hazards are the crumbling cliffs and the rising sea. **Keep well away from the cliff edge** when traversing the precipices and don't attempt to climb on them from the beach. There are times when the path can be claimed by the waves so if signs are posted advising you not to continue do follow their warning. Tidal conditions and any flood alerts can be checked before starting out by calling Great Yarmouth Coastguard or visiting the Maritime and Coastguard Agency website (see Appendix B).

Bikes are not permitted on most of the coast section of the Peddars Way and Norfolk Coast Path so leave them at home. Much of the inland part of the Peddars Way can be cycled, however, and the Norfolk Coast Cycleway, which links King's Lynn and Great Yarmouth, passes through some of the villages encountered on the Norfolk Coast Path (see www.norfolkcoastaonb.org.uk).

Maps

There is no single map for the whole route so a combination of several is needed to cover the entire trail. These can be purchased at local tourist information centres (see Appendix B).

- OS Explorer (1:25,000)
  229, 236, 250, 251 and 252
- OS Landranger (1:50,000)
  132, 133 and 144

EMERGENCIES

For the most part mobile phone reception is good, and a village or town where further help is available is never too far away. In emergencies call 999; a number of emergency phones are situated at various points along the coast. If you need help when on the

cliffs or beach dial 999 but ask for the Coastguard. Remember to take your own personalised first aid kit with you when walking, including any necessary medication.

USING THIS GUIDE

Whether planning to walk the whole 155km (96-mile) National Trail in one, or intending to break it up into shorter one-, two- or three-day sections, or split it into a complete traverse of the Peddars Way section first, followed by a separate walk on the Norfolk Coast Path, this book will enable you to plan your trip.

The complete long-distance path has been divided into eight stages. These have been chosen to offer a good day of walking with easily accessible start and finish points that take advantage of towns and villages with good transport links, accommodation options and amenities. They, of course, do not have to be followed in their entirety as presented. If you intend only to do the 76km (47-mile) coastal section then Stages 5–8 can be followed, and if you want to complete the 79km (49-mile) Peddars Way then simply do Stages 1–4.

Within each stage there is information on potential overnight stops, as well as recommended attractions to visit. There is also advice on local public transport options, and bus stops are noted for each start and finish point.

Timings

At the start of each stage an approximate time for completing it is given. As walkers go at different speeds this has been calculated using Naismith's Rule (allowing 1 hour per 4km, plus an extra 10mins per 100m of ascent and 30mins for breaks for every 4 hours' walking). Use these as a guide only as they are based on someone walking to get the distance covered; remember that time spent enjoying the spectacular scenery can really add up, and that walking on sand/shingle requires more effort and will therefore take longer than walking on woodland trails or tarmac.

British beach huts at their best at Wells-next-the-Sea (Stage 6)

GETTING THERE

As with any linear path, getting to the start and away from the end of the route easily is key. Unless you intend to use two cars (and it is not recommended that you leave a car unattended for several days), then public transport is the best option. If you intend to walk the whole National Trail then your start/finish points are Knettishall Heath, Suffolk, and Cromer, Norfolk.

Knettishall Heath is reached from Thetford (accessed by rail with connections to London, Cambridge and Norwich) either by taxi (costing around £15 in 2012) or, if you go midweek, the Brecks Bus which operates from the train station (around £2 per person). To use this service book in advance by calling 01638 608080, giving at least 48 hours' notice (you can give up to, but no more than, two weeks' notice if you wish). If you want to stay the night before you start walking then your best option is Thetford. There are several options here including B&Bs, inns and hotels (visit www.explorethetford.co.uk or see the National Trail website in Appendix B).

Cromer is reached by train, bus or coach. In 2012 it was possible to book a ticket from London King's Cross that took you all the way via train and bus. Cromer is well connected with London and Cambridge, from where other national services can be accessed.

If you plan to add a break in between the inland Peddars Way

The Coasthopper bus serves all the villages and towns on the Norfolk Coast Path between Hunstanton and Cromer.

section and the Norfolk Coast Path stages then Hunstanton is the obvious choice. There are regular buses from the main bus station to King's Lynn train station from where connections on to Ely, Cambridge and London can be made (then onwards to the rest of the rail network).

GETTING AROUND

The Norfolk Coast Path section is undoubtedly the easiest one to access at virtually any point via public transport. The Coasthopper bus, operated by Norfolk Green, is a great tool for cutting this 76km (47-mile) stretch into the four stages described in this book, or for shorter or longer variations to suit your level of fitness and

available time. It also offers an escape route should the weather turn bad at any point and you wish to call it a day. Different tickets are available (see Stage 5, 'Transport links on the Norfolk Coast Path'), depending on your needs.

The Peddars Way (79km/49 miles) can be a trickier part of the National Trail to split up. Walking it in its entirety over four days is recommended, purely for simplicity. There are local services to some of the villages at the end of Stages 1, 2 and 3, but these are infrequent and it is highly recommended to check the most current timetables on www.traveline.org.uk rather than assuming that a particular service is still operational.

WHEN TO GO

Luckily the Peddars Way and Norfolk Coast Path is a walk that can be enjoyed year round. In the summer it can feel akin to walking abroad with big blue skies and the best of the British seaside at your doorstep. However, at this time of year the region – in particular the coastal section – is a huge draw for nearby city folk who want to escape for some much-needed fresh air, so the sections through larger villages and towns can be particularly busy with both walkers and visitors. It is a fantastic time to go, but pre-booking accommodation is vital if you want to be assured of a bed.

In winter the path takes on a whole new character. Icy easterly winds can make the coastal stretches feel almost arctic; in some years snow falls on the sand dunes, and the path becomes frozen. The advantage of walking in these conditions is that the crowds are gone and the journey can feel much more epic than in high season. The downside is the reduced hours of daylight for completing each stage, which can be something of a challenge. On top of that a fair few accommodation providers shut up shop at this time of year, limiting your options and causing those who do ride it out year round to book up quicker than usual – especially on weekends – so again booking ahead is advised for peace of mind.

No matter what the weather the entire path is one to savour. If you have the time try and experience it in both seasons to really get a flavour of the place.

IN WHICH DIRECTION?

It is up to you to work out which direction is best for you. This book describes the Peddars Way section first – from south to north – then the Norfolk Coast Path section from west to east. One reason for this is that the hardest part to get to (via public transport) is dealt with upfront. Also walking towards the sea seems to feel like a journey with a real purpose. For the Romans and Iceni – in whose footsteps you are treading – it was a major destination, somehow making it feel like the right way to go.

All in one go?

Some long-distance walkers are purists when it comes to walking a National Trail, believing that the whole thing should be walked in one to make it a 'true' experience. However, it is important to enjoy the landscape you're passing through, rather than just putting your head down and getting on with it. If time won't allow you to do it in one trip then breaking it up makes it no less of an adventure.

Splitting it into the eight sections described in this book over a series of weekends or one-day trips – no doubt experiencing different weather each time – can really spice up the route, offering a glimpse of it in different

The cluster of beach huts on the beachfront at Old Hunstanton more usually seen
in summer sunshine, take on a different – yet still attractive – guise in the depths of
winter (Stage 4)

Yurts and tepees on the Norfolk skyline at the campsite in Burnham Deepdale (Stage 5)

conditions. Completing it will still be a triumphant moment.

ACCOMMODATION

There is a whole mixture of places to stay along the entire path to suit all budgets and preferences. It's just as plausible to do the whole walk staying in a tent in campsites as it is having every night in the comfort of B&Bs or hotels. As with public transport, the Norfolk Coast Path section offers the most choice and, due to the Coasthopper bus, enables you to base yourself in one location and tick off the whole thing without moving on each night if preferred.

Each stage in the book offers advice on local towns and villages, including their available accommodation options. For the latest information on this see www.nationaltrail.co.uk and click on the interactive accommodation map or download the trail companion as a printable PDF, which lists not only available places but also gives information on how far off-path they are – an aspect not to be underestimated.

HEALTH AND SAFETY

Most of the time on this path, help, should it be needed, is not that far away. As with any trip, if walking alone consider leaving a route card with a responsible person, including details of where you plan to stay and the date and approximate time you intend to be back, so that they can raise the alarm if you fail to show up. Take the regular precautions you would on any walk: carry your mobile phone, a map and compass (and know how to use them), a personalised first aid kit and use your judgement – for example, if you are taking longer than expected on a section don't be afraid to alter your plans. The biggest hazard will be some of the road sections on the Peddars Way, so stay alert for traffic when walking along these.

PRACTICALITIES

Food and drink
On the coast you can pick up any supplies you need as you go (although carrying enough water for your day's walk and some snacks, such as cereal bars, is definitely recommended). On the Peddars Way it is better to pick up supplies in the town or village where you stay overnight in preparation for the next day's walking. Information on where food is available is given in each of the stages.

Money (ATMs)
As you'll be going through some fairly small villages and many businesses prefer to deal in cash, it is best to take enough with you – particularly for the Peddars Way section. The halfway point at Hunstanton is a good place for replenishing funds if needed, and Cromer and Thetford (for Knettishall Heath) have cashpoints.

Post, phones and internet
Despite some places on the route being merely hamlets most do boast a postbox, which means 'keeping it traditional' by sending postcards to friends is possible. Most also have phone boxes, although mobile reception is good throughout this route so taking yours (even turned off, except in emergencies) is advised. The internet – from which you might like to take a break! – is only available in the larger towns such as Hunstanton and Cromer, but may be offered in certain places.

A little taste of a classic English village: Thornham, near Holme next the Sea (Stage 5)

A howling good view – the wooden sculpture at St Edmund's Chapel at dusk

STAGE 1
Knettishall Heath to Little Cressingham

Start	Car park opposite Blackwater Carr, Knettishall Heath (TL 943 807)
Finish	Crossroads in Little Cressingham (TF 873 000)
Distance	23.5km (14½ miles)
Time	6½hrs
Refreshments	Pubs and cafés in Thetford; Dog and Partridge PH, Stonebridge; Windmill Inn, Great Cressingham (off-route)
Toilets	At car park/rest area 6km after start
Public transport	Brecks bus from Thetford station; infrequent buses from Little Cressingham to Watton, Threxton and Attleborough, with connections to King's Lynn; bus from Stonebridge to Thetford
Parking	Knettishall Heath; limited on-street parking in Little Cressingham
Accommodation	B&Bs, hotels and hostels in Thetford; B&B in Little Cressingham and Great Cressingham (off-route)

After a fleeting foray into Suffolk on the first few steps of this National Trail you will be plunged into Norfolk's Breckland landscape with its trademark Scots pines. This forest scenery accompanies most of this stage, interspersed with the occasional glimpse of the wide-open spaces that this county is famed for. Keep a lookout for the skittish muntjac deer and the first few art installations that line the Peddars Way, and steal a look into the secretive military land that borders your journey and is closed to all but the MOD.

▶ The walk starts with very little fanfare: a signpost opposite the car park simply stating 'Peddars Way'. Here you're informed that approximately 46 miles separate you from Holme next the Sea where you will join the Norfolk Coast Path section of the National Trail. There are a few stages between now and then so take your first steps through the gate and for the next few minutes enjoy your brief foray in Suffolk. Trees stretch above on either

It's advisable to pick lunch up in Thetford before you start. There is nowhere guaranteed to offer food on the path, particularly out of season.

Map continues on
page 34

side as you head north before following the path over a small footbridge. The water beneath is the Little Ouse River and marks your transition into Norfolk.

Here the path bears northeast before swinging north again. In winter patches of snowdrops line the track as you skirt along the trees and pass fields of pigs on your left-hand side. Keep your eyes peeled as hares often tear across the path ahead. Before reaching the A1066, in the last field on the right, look out for a metal pipe that drops into the ground for several metres. This is part of an elaborate irrigation system that keeps the typically sandy Breckland soil damp when it is too dry to produce crops.

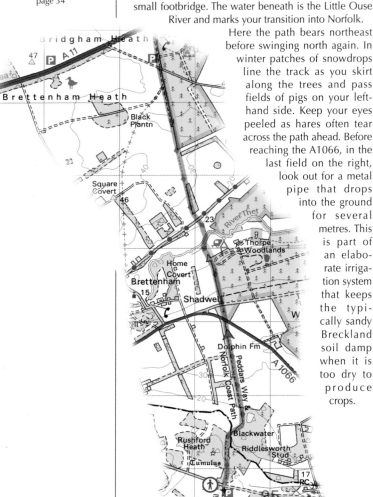

Continue on to cross the A1066, taking care as cars come pretty fast along here. Follow the path through more trees then cross the minor road into **Thorpe Woodlands**. From this point on it's worth keeping alert in case you spot a muntjac deer. These dog-like small mammals have a tendency to dart out from the trees before jumping back in again before you've managed to get your camera ready! Through the trees on the right – much easier to spot – are usually some tents or caravans in the Forestry Commission's campsite. ▶

Soon the path emerges from the trees onto open fields to reach a handy wooden boardwalk (watch out when wet as it gets very slippery) above the often boggy fields and on to the **River Thet**. Swans and ducks tend to congregate in these waters as you edge the banks on the wooden slats. A bridge takes you over the river. Continue ahead, now on a dirt track to cross the Brettenham road.

Meander through the trees at Broom Covert and along the edge of farmland. Continue through an area of lowland heath owned and managed by Natural England and one of the largest areas of heathland in the Brecks.

Crossing the Little Ouse River, the boundary between Suffolk and Norfolk at Knettishall Heath

A good start point for this section if you want to walk the path and camp along the way.

31

Taking the boardwalk alongside the River Thet near Thorpe Farm

Brettenham Heath Nature Reserve is predominantly a combination of acid grassland, chalk grassland and heather heathland and features a number of Scots pine that are characteristic of this part of Norfolk. The area has an interesting archaeology: there is evidence of what is believed to be a post-medieval stock enclosure, and a Neolithic stone flake was also found here in 1985.

Several species of birds can be spotted in this habitat including curlew, redstart and buzzard. It is also said that it has the lowest rainfall of anywhere in the UK, so fingers crossed this holds true when you visit! It is worth noting that from March to October is the breeding season, so access is restricted (the Peddars Way is not affected). For more information see www.naturalengland.org.uk and click on National Nature Reserves.

Continue along the path and soon you'll start to hear the hum of the cars on the nearby A11 road. Just before reaching it there's a handy place to stop on the right. It's a rest area for cars and usually has a coffee/snack bar year-round, as well as toilets.

After a quick break continue north, taking great care when crossing the main road. Once safely on the other side you'll get a real taste of things to come in the shape of a notice on the left – 'Military Training: Keep Out' – a prominent feature on this stage of the Peddars Way.

Carry on to the railway line (Ely–Norwich) and cross via a gate, making sure to listen carefully for oncoming trains before going. ▶

A few steps later another path veers off to the left. This is an old drove road that is thought to predate the Roman one you're walking on. From here this so-called Great Fen Road (the Hereward Way) stretches off into the distance, passing several meres (drinking places) on the way. As Breckland is often short of water these ancient throughways were plotted to take in such vital sources to refresh weary travellers.

For a safer, alternative route turn right just before the line; after a few metres find the entrance to a tunnel on your left and pass under the railway.

To continue on your way ignore this path (perhaps save it for another day) and carry straight on. Pass through more woods to reach the gas pipeline pumping station, a fairly pungent-smelling place! Here the track feels like more of a minor road than the dirt tracks you've been following thus far. There are remains of an old dismantled railway to the left of the path, formerly the Thetford–Watton line. Far more visible are the horses and donkeys in the fields round about. Carry on ahead to reach the two abutments of an old railway bridge where the path continues to a road.

Cross the road in front of you and turn right; in a few steps you'll emerge into the village of **Stonebridge** where buses are available (in 2012 service 81 Monday to Friday, operated by Coach Services, www.coachservice-sltd.com) to take you back to Thetford should you want to break your journey here and come back another day. Otherwise, continue on through the village. There is more evidence that you are heading deeper into military country with a number of signs forbidding military vehicles from driving down the roads. Walk along the pavement, passing the Dog and Partridge pub (food served all day

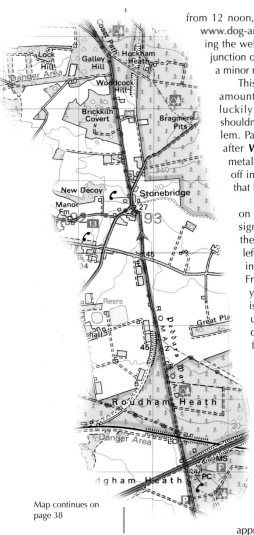

from 12 noon, accommodation available, www.dog-and-partridge.org.uk), following the well-marked signs north. At the junction of the main Thetford road and a minor road, bear left on the latter.

This next section involves a fair amount of road walking, though luckily it is relatively quiet so shouldn't prove too much of a problem. Pass some houses and a little after **Woodcock Hill** you'll see a metalled road on the left veering off into the trees. This is the road that leads to the military base.

Ignore this turn-off and carry on following the National Trail signs. A little after **Galley Hill** the more defined road swings left while you bear right following signs for the Peddars Way. From this point on prepare yourself. All the land to the left is owned by the MOD and is used for military training 350 days of the year. For the next few kilometres you will hear gunfire and explosions, and may see tanks and soldiers appearing on either side of the track. It's certainly an odd backdrop in an otherwise tranquil area.

Still it does add interest to the walk as you catch glimpses of a world that will, for now, remain a mystery to us civvies. Note that **Watering Farm** is marked on the OS map approximately 1.5km north from

Map continues on page 38

34

MILITARY PRESENCE ON THE PEDDARS WAY

Behind the secretive fences and gates and their 'No Entry' signs to the west of the Peddars Way sits a deserted village called Tottington. Taken over (along with the villages of Buckenham Tofts, Langford, Stanford, Sturston and West Tofts) by the Army during World War II it was incorporated into the Stanford Battle Area (established 1942) and used as part of a 30,000-acre training ground to prepare forces for the Battle of Normandy in 1944. Understandably not all the residents were happy to leave – to hear a perspective from one such villager it is worth checking out *Farming, on a Battle Ground* by A Norfolk Woman (aka Lucille Reeve).

Warning signs line the first stage of the path from the A11 to Home Farm near Merton – do not cross!

Despite the end of the war in 1945 no one was ever allowed to go back to the village again. The government took over the land under threat of a compulsory purchase order – going back on a promise they had made – leaving many villagers with no farms and no homes. Although they fought to return, events surrounding the Cold War meant there was no hope of them going back. The village became a dedicated training ground owned by the Ministry of Defence.

Access is strictly out of bounds and walking on this section of the National Trail you will often hear the explosions and shots carried on the wind from inside the boundaries. But it is said that in what was Tottington the church is still standing. You may have seen glimpses of it – other than while walking this section of path – on the TV series *Dad's Army* since it was used as a location for scenes when the Home Guard went on exercises.

the fork at Galley Hill. The place holds little significance other than it means a number of trucks utilise this section of the track to access it, so care is needed. Aside from being aware of approaching vehicles, it is worth noting that the tyre tracks can create large grooves which are

Expect to see and hear evidence of military activity while on this woodland track shortly after leaving Stonebridge

very muddy or waterlogged particularly after a spell of bad weather. Once you've passed the turn-off to the farm you can relax as the path is blocked to vehicular access by concrete boulders.

This is another spot where it's worth keeping the camera ready in case you spot a deer. Bizarrely they seem at home with gunfire, though are still very jumpy around walkers! Continuing along the path you'll notice the first of one of five of the Norfolk Songlines stones that line the trail sporadically from here until the sea is reached (see 'Arts' in the Introduction). This one bears the

The first of five Norfolk Songlines sculptures by Tom Perkins that dot the Peddars Way

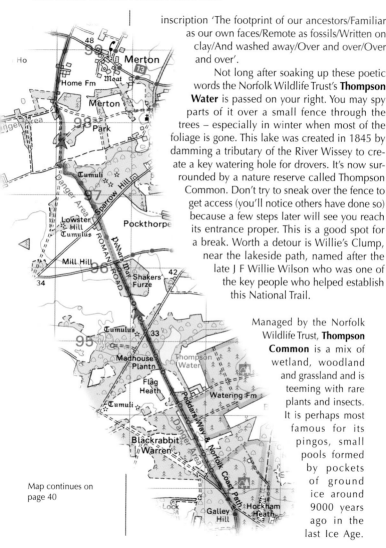

inscription 'The footprint of our ancestors/Familiar as our own faces/Remote as fossils/Written on clay/And washed away/Over and over/Over and over'.

Not long after soaking up these poetic words the Norfolk Wildlife Trust's **Thompson Water** is passed on your right. You may spy parts of it over a small fence through the trees – especially in winter when most of the foliage is gone. This lake was created in 1845 by damming a tributary of the River Wissey to create a key watering hole for drovers. It's now surrounded by a nature reserve called Thompson Common. Don't try to sneak over the fence to get access (you'll notice others have done so) because a few steps later will see you reach its entrance proper. This is a good spot for a break. Worth a detour is Willie's Clump, near the lakeside path, named after the late J F Willie Wilson who was one of the key people who helped establish this National Trail.

Managed by the Norfolk Wildlife Trust, **Thompson Common** is a mix of wetland, woodland and grassland and is teeming with rare plants and insects. It is perhaps most famous for its pingos, small pools formed by pockets of ground ice around 9000 years ago in the last Ice Age.

Map continues on page 40

For a closer look a 12.75km (8-mile) circular walking route, the Great Eastern Pingo Trail, tours these
geological phenomena. This is worth checking out
if you are staying a little longer in the area or are
feeling especially energetic and fancy adding it
onto your route. For more information visit www.
norfolkwildlifetrust.org.uk and click on Nature
Reserves.

*The second of the
five Norfolk Songlines
sculptures appears
just before Merton
Park*

Continue on the path as the trees begin to thin
and soon, near the Cherryrow Plantation, you'll see a
minor road on the right that leads to Pockthorpe. Here is
another handy place to stop for a snack as several more
concrete boulders block the track to traffic and provide
ample benches for a weary walker. Otherwise cross this
minor road and continue on, with fewer trees now lining the path. When you head back into the woods again
you'll pass behind the Merton estate owned by Lord
Walsingham who helped open up this particular stretch
of the long-distance route.

Just after passing the second Norfolk Songlines sculpture – bearing the quote Surveyors have made their lines
on the land/Trapping Albion in a net of roads/A taut web
on the edge of empire – look out for warning signs about

the giant hogweed rising above the path. The sap causes irritation and burns to the skin that can last for several days and can even result in blindness if contact is made with the eyes. In winter it's not so much of an issue, but in summer care is definitely needed – especially if bringing children with you.

Passing the sculpture marks the end of the neighbouring military presence; the MOD land branches off to the left at Blackbreck Covert to the east while your path heads north, passing **Home Farm**, the first proper residence seen in a while. Stick to the path, which is now more of a dirt and gravel road, passing between farm buildings to reach a crossroads.

Here a sign will advise of the distance to establishments in the nearby village of **Merton**. It's certainly an option for accommodation (currently there is one B&B) – especially when other places are full in high season – but bear in mind a return journey will add 1km to your route. If you're not planning this detour take the signposted left turn onto a grassy track. Follow this along the edges of fields, lined with arching trees, then turn right to follow the path up and along to the Brandon road (B1108).

Cross this. It's not immediately obvious from the signage whether the path goes along the fast-moving road on the steep embankment or in the field behind it, but it is, thankfully, in the field. So turn left, keeping to the track on the edge of farmland with the hedge to the left. It stays behind this for most of the way now, occasionally signposted to move onto the road side of the hedge, though luckily on a wide grassy verge.

Finally the welcome sight of the village sign for **Little Cressingham** comes into view ahead. Make sure you stick to the right-hand road at the fork and walk down carefully into the village. At the crossroads turn right to reach its very quiet centre.

LITTLE CRESSINGHAM

Little Cressingham is a small but pleasant village. It may, as its moniker suggests, be lacking in size but it is a settlement that is scattered across the surrounding countryside. Points of interest include the Grade-I-listed church of St Andrew and the disused Grade-II-listed water and windmill. Sadly the village pub – The White Horse – closed in 2004.

It is worth noting that there is a bus stop in Little Cressingham with a very infrequent service to Watton, Threxton or Attleborough, from where onward links go to a number of towns including King's Lynn (see Appendix B). There is some (admittedly limited) potential to break your journey here if you want to do Stage 1 as a single day. However, waiting until the end of Stage 2 is a better option.

Accommodation options are a little limited. The only one directly en route is at the crossroads: the friendly Sycamore House B&B, used to attending to tired trail walkers. They offer a number of rooms, with private or shared facilities, and a fabulous hearty cooked breakfast to fuel you up for the next day's walk. Included in the stay is a lift to and from the Windmill Inn in Great Cressingham where you can grab your evening meal! For more information about the village check out www.ltcressinghamandthrexton.org.uk.

There are other overnight options in Great Cressingham but they are some distance off the path and, by this time, the thought of any extra kilometres – even just a couple – can be really off-putting! More information about other options is available from the National Trail office and free from the website at www.nationaltrail.co.uk.

STAGE 2
Little Cressingham to Castle Acre

Start	Crossroads in Little Cressingham (TF 873 000)
Finish	Bailey Gate, Castle Acre (TF 817 151)
Distance	19km (11¾ miles)
Time	5½hrs
Refreshments	Blue Lion PH, Pickenham; McDonald's, A47 near Swaffham; tearooms and The Feathers PH, Castle Acre
Toilets	In petrol station on A47
Public transport	Infrequent buses from Castle Acre to Swaffham and King's Lynn
Parking	Limited on-street parking in Castle Acre, public car park by castle
Accommodation	B&Bs and hotel in Castle Acre

Quiet country lanes ease you into this stage of the journey, typified by a smattering of chalk-encased flint in the surrounding fields that is also evident in the village buildings passed. A tree-lined avenue takes you one step closer to Castle Acre, the pièce de résistance on the Peddars Way. Officially the path moves through this town fairly directly, offering only tantalising views of the Norman Cluniac priory, Bailey Gate and motte-and-bailey castle. But here, after a shorter day's hike, there is time to explore these historic sites and learn more about earlier users of the path.

The first section of Stage 2 follows minor country roads, so the going is straightforward and relatively easy, but watch out for vehicles that may be sharing it with you.

◄ Turn right at the crossroads in **Little Cressingham** to continue north on the Peddars Way. The first couple of kilometres out of the village offer something in the way of grass verges which make for much safer walking. Where this is not possible walk on the right side of the road, facing any oncoming traffic.

After crossing the Great Cressingham road the lane is less frequented so you can relax a little. Continue straight on, heading towards the South Pickenham–Ashill road. As the trees begin to thin look to your left as you may be able to spot glimpses of the imposing **Pickenham Hall**, built in 1903, its vast array of windows staring back at you like a cluster of mirrored eyes. Don't get too distracted though, as soon the main road is reached.

Map continues on page 46

Go straight across it – watching out for any fast vehicles – and continue uphill. Take care as the road narrows and bends; for the next few hundred metres there is no way of getting off the road to let cars pass. Thankfully at Houghton Carr the path is diverted left off the road behind a hedge – it's a great relief to be standing in a field! Make sure to stick to the top of this, near the hedge (this is private land, and in summer can be home to livestock), and cross the farm track to carry straight on, still walking along the top of the meadow. At the hedge turn left, descending to the River Wissey. Here turn right again following the bank alongside the water in a northerly direction.

This particular section of the path is littered with splinters of churned-up flint. Look at the soil beneath your feet and you'll see hundreds of white flecks scattered across it. Some will be beige, others black or cream; you

43

Shards of flint litter the fields on the first part of Stage 2 on the Peddars Way

may even find some shards encased in chalk, resembling dinosaur teeth or bones at first glance.

Resulting from chemical changes within compressed sedimentary rock, **flint** is found usually as nodules inside other sedimentary rock such as chalk and limestone. It is dark in appearance with shades of green, black or grey being most common. Textually it feels almost like a piece of glass, smooth and sometimes waxy, but on the outside it usually has a thin layer of white that is rough to the touch.

It is found in many places around the UK but especially in Norfolk and on the South Coast. On the Peddars Way it is evident as small splinters ploughed up by farmers tending their land, but occasionally you may spot giant blocks. As you progress further on the trail you will also notice that the local houses are built from this naturally occurring material, hardly surprising considering its abundance in the area. It was popular with the Romans who used it, along with other stones and mortar, to build forts. When used as a building material it can look very decorative, and gives some of the villages passed through their own distinct character.

When you get to a patch of trees and sunken ground, and can go no further, take the path branching off left to a stile. Cross this and continue straight ahead to take a small footbridge across the river.

On the other side head to the corner of the field. Once there, turn right following the path through the fields, crossing stiles, until it turns left alongside a hedge towards a school. At the corner of the field turn right, then left at the fenceline, and onwards up towards the road (the school will be on the left). This is the small village of **North Pickenham**. Turn right and follow the road into the centre.

Although there is a bus stop here that you can use to reach Swaffham there is very little else in the way of amenities. A wooden statue marks the central point from where the main road curves down to the Blue Lion pub (http://thebluelionpub.co.uk). This hostelry is only open in the evening but does not serve food. ▶ There is no general store or anywhere to buy sandwiches or snacks, but there is chance to do this in another couple of kilometres.

It is worth noting that the Blue Lion (2012) offers its beer garden overnight for free to those walking and camping.

On last inspection the Peddars Way signs were broken in this village but the route is easy to find. Simply turn left down the main road heading uphill (walking away from the statue and pub). Unfortunately the path follows the tarmac for this section (the grass verge is too high and too steep to be of much use) so exercise caution.

You'll soon hear the roar of vehicles on a go-karting track to the left as the verge to the right lowers and becomes usable. Further left you may have noticed a collection of wind turbines. These are on a former World War II airfield, which for three months was base to the American 492nd Bomb Group. For a short while the skies above would have been filled with the roar of B-24 Liberators. After the war the RAF took over the site and caused some controversy in 1959 when it was revealed to be home to ballistic nuclear missiles. After many protests and public outcry the weapons were moved, and now just an ironically rocket-shaped structure amid the giant eight turbines gives a hint of its former use.

Continue on to reach the Swaffham–Holme Hale road. Cross this to reach a gate and a sign advising that passage is not open to motorised vehicles – good news for walkers! Go through the gate to find a tree-lined path. This can be muddy, particularly after heavy rain, but sticking to its edges can help. This is a very old part of the Peddars Way known as Procession Lane, believed to be a reference to the ancient Beating of the Bounds ceremony.

The origins of **Beating of the Bounds** go back centuries before maps were commonplace. It was a tradition that saw members of a community, every year – usually on Ascension Day – process along the boundary of a parish, lead by the priest, and beat the border markers with boughs of willow. This would help people remember where parish boundaries were so that the information could be shared and passed on through the generations and so discourage neighbouring parishes from moving markers and claiming some of their land. The community would pray for the protection of the parish boundary and bless the landscape, often singing hymns. Some think the tradition came

Map continues on page 50

Grange Fm

58

ROMAN ROAD

Peddars

Way

77

Petygards

Karting

37

Manor Fm

PH North Pickenham

38

Meadow Fm

53

45

57

48

from a Roman celebration to the god of landmarks called Terminus where people would drink, dance and celebrate at boundary lines. The Beating of the Bounds is still observed in parts of England and Wales to this day.

Now the National Trail follows an oblique line in a northwesterly direction, almost dye straight, very indicative of a true Roman road. You'll notice the abutments of a former railway bridge near the start of this lane, all that is left here of the railway line that in 1875 used to link Thetford (near the start of this walk) and Swaffham (4km northwest of this point). Carry straight on, and shortly after keeping ahead at a crossroads of paths you'll spot another of the Norfolk Songlines sculptures on the right, bearing the inscription 'The piety of every man and every woman's whispered prayer/Clasped in the grain of wood and stone and in the grace of ancient air'. It offers a pensive spot to enjoy the tranquillity before reaching the frenetic activity on the A47 ahead.

When you reach this road be very careful crossing it as the cars and some very large articulated lorries race by

Horses graze the fields near Meadow Farm, North Pickenham

The tree-lined path leading out of North Pickenham is known as Procession Lane

at 60mph. If you were hoping for somewhere to grab a bite to eat you've found it! Once on the other side of the road, less than 100m to the left, is a service station and McDonald's restaurant offering drinks and snacks and the chance to use the bathroom without having to divert far from the path.

When ready to move on follow the path, now more of a country lane, past **Grange Farm** and up and over the remains of yet another railway line, this time the defunct King's Lynn–Dereham track. Here the path swings round to the left to meet the Sporle road. Turn right onto it and follow it to the first turning on the left. Go down this minor road, heading north again past the line of houses.

To the west is the impressive **Palgrave Hall** that can just about be made out through the trees on the left. Follow the track straight on, continuing down the dirt road towards the farm buildings. As you reach the farm look to the field on the left to see a series of lumps and bumps, the remains of the medieval village of Great Palgrave. Stop for a second; look closely and you can make out the foundations of the houses and structures that once would have stood here.

Continue on to meet South Acre Road. Turn left and follow it along (keeping the farm to your right). It's a short trudge on the tarmac road before the path branches off left to pass behind the hedge. There is a large tree trunk blocking the National Trail to motorised vehicles, which can make a handy place to sit and enjoy a drink. Continue on the track following the hedgeline, descending on grass. Where the hedge ends stay on the grassy verge for as long as possible until it becomes easier to

The third of the Norfolk Songlines sculptures, this one triangular in shape, is found on the Peddars Way near Swaffham

cross over onto the verge on the other side of the road; follow this all the way to the A1065.

This is a wide road and the vehicles go very fast, so take care when crossing. Once on the other side, take the road ahead signposted to **South Acre**. Ignore the track that veers off to the left and continue on the tarmac heading uphill. Once you've reached something of a high point the road sweeps down to the right. Follow it downhill to a crossroads. Go straight ahead (the now familiar acorn emblems on the telegraph poles confirm you're on the right track) passing Church Farm, which is on the right. After the buildings end the road bends round to the right (much narrower and very little used by vehicles). Go with it – you'll be getting ever-more impressive views of the remains of the Clunaic priory to the left – and continue down to the ford, crossed via a footbridge.

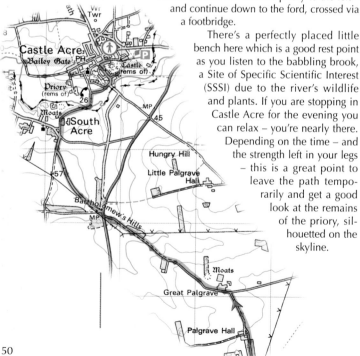

There's a perfectly placed little bench here which is a good rest point as you listen to the babbling brook, a Site of Specific Scientific Interest (SSSI) due to the river's wildlife and plants. If you are stopping in Castle Acre for the evening you can relax – you're nearly there. Depending on the time – and the strength left in your legs – this is a great point to leave the path temporarily and get a good look at the remains of the priory, silhouetted on the skyline.

An exploration of the Cluniac priory at Castle Acre is a must

CASTLE ACRE PRIORY

Dramatic and beautiful, the remains of one of England's best-preserved monastic sites is a sight for sore eyes for walkers on the Peddars Way. Not only does it mark something of a halfway point on this inland section of the National Trail, but it also gives a good excuse to leave the path for a while. From the sky-lit arches to the twisted ruins of spiral staircases and the frames of old windows that would have overlooked the cloister, it is a fascinating place. It is not hard to imagine how it would have looked in its former glory.

The building dates back to 1090AD and, after an earlier smaller priory within the walls of the nearby castle was deemed too small and inconvenient, it became home to the first Cluniac Order of 20–30 monks. There they lived for hundreds of years until the priory's dissolution in 1537 when King Henry VIII gave it to the Duke of Norfolk, who turned out the last remaining monks. It is now owned by the Earl of Leicester and is under the care of English Heritage.

To pay the priory a visit go through the gap in the wall behind the bench and follow the path that keeps to the left of the field, flush to the water, before branching north safely through boggy ground and up to the perimeter fence of the ruins. Trace their edge uphill to the visitor centre on the left, where there are exhibitions and artefacts to study before heading into the grounds.

To return to the trail retrace your steps back to the hole in the wall and turn left at the bench.

Continue along the water's edge at first, then follow the now more road-like path to the left, steadily climbing uphill. Where the road forks right follow it to the main road into **Castle Acre**. Turn left and climb uphill into town. At the top of the road you'll see the Bailey Gate – a huge stone arch that once would have marked the entrance to the town.

Seeing as Stage 2 is a little shorter than Stage 3 give yourself time at the end of this stage to visit the nearby castle. Once through the gate (watch out for cars), turn right on the road and follow signs towards the castle. You would be forgiven for thinking that this small Norfolk village would be an unlikely spot in which to find a castle – even a small one. But there is and small it certainly is not, as you will discover when you turn the corner and see it standing before you.

Founded shortly after the 1066 Norman Conquest (and rebuilt in the 1140s) **Castle Acre Castle** is strategically sited at the point where the Peddars Way crosses the River Nar, a key location for controlling those travelling to the town and also bringing supplies by river, itself a natural defence.

It is of motte-and-bailey design, with the lord's house on the motte, most protected from attack, and the bailey area below occupied by the shops and homes of the community. There are inner and outer walls as well as walkways and gates (one of which is still partially standing), all of which help to create an extra-secure stronghold. The castle, priory and Bailey Gate are all under the care of English Heritage (see Appendix B).

The remains of the 11th-century castle at Castle Acre: a great place to visit in this charming village

CASTLE ACRE

There are plenty of accommodation options in Castle Acre, including several B&Bs and a hostel (up-to-date details available from the National Trail website, see Appendix B). Not all are open outside the summer season, so phone ahead to check rather than turning up on the off chance.

Two tearooms (both on Stocks Green) are open during the day, offering homemade cakes and light meals as well as hot and cold drinks. There is a general store on the route of the Peddars Way where you can stock up on sandwiches and snacks for the next day's walking.

The village pub – The Feathers – serves a range of locally sourced dishes in the evening (booking recommended, particularly on weekends), real ales and wines, perfect for post-walking gluttony and socialising! More local information can be found at http://www.castleacre.net.

A bus runs to nearby Swaffham, Monday to Friday, but is very infrequent. Three buses a week go to King's Lynn (2012), which is handy for those wanting to break the walk up into single days or combine Stages 1 and 2 (see Appendix B).

The remains of Cluniac Priory greet walkers at Castle Acre

STAGE 3
Castle Acre to Sedgeford

Start	Bailey Gate, Castle Acre (TF 817 151)
Finish	B1454, Sedgeford (TF 722 368)
Distance	24.25km (15 miles)
Time	6½hrs
Refreshments	The King William IV Country Inn, Sedgeford
Toilets	No pubic toilets on route
Public transport	Infrequent buses from Sedgeford to Hunstanton
Parking	Limited on-street parking in Sedgeford
Accommodation	B&B and hotel in Sedgeford

Time to get your head down and crack through the kilometres on the first stretch of this stage, where, despite the views being less impressive than on Stages 1 and 2, one of the highest points above sea level on the route is reached. Once that hurdle is overcome Bronze Age tumuli and old marl pits dot the open fields flanking the trail. Here the words 'big skies' – often bandied about when it comes to Norfolk – really start to mean something. The day ends in the village of Sedgeford, where a friendly pub awaits before you edge closer to the coast.

From **Castle Acre** High Street, before reaching the castle, turn left to follow the Great Massingham road, passing a general store where you can buy a sandwich, snacks and drinks for the stage ahead. ▶ From the shop continue straight ahead, on the pavement at first and ignoring any turn-offs to reach the last few houses of the village. After the pavement ends and the last of the cottages and the minor road that turns off left have been passed, the route thankfully goes behind the hedge on the left and skirts the road in the safety of a field. Look back occasionally to catch sight of Castle Acre which, from a distance, can be appreciated in its entirety. Follow the path to Old Wicken Cottages when, unfortunately, the route re-joins the road.

The first section of Stage 3 is a bit of a trudge along a minor road for about 4.5km – uphill.

The trig point that denotes one of the Peddars Way highs sits after the climb from Little Cressingham

An alternative option for accommodation if you are breaking the route up into smaller sections or fancy a longer day on Stage 2 – see www. greatmassingham.net.

Cross the stile to reach the tarmac. Follow the road as it heads northwest, taking care to look out for any fast-moving cars. As the road starts to descend there is a path on the grassy verge on the left side. Continue on this until the crossroads where the verge path switches to the right-hand side of the road. Carefully cross over and follow the verge uphill.

Soon the road bends round to the right. Here you'll spot an Ordnance Survey trig point on the left side of the road, marking the 92m contour. Cross over to reach this, one of the highest points on this long-distance route. The road heads off towards the picturesque village of **Great Massingham** about 1.5km off the path. ◄ The National Trail continues in a straight line northwest, forking off left from the road.

Follow it along a muddy track, negotiating the ruts made by farm vehicles and horses, which cuts downhill. You'll undoubtedly start to hear the cries of gulls overhead as you soon pass through a massive pig farm. See how they peer at you, looking for food, while the scavenger seagulls lurk overhead, also hopeful of scraps.

Map continues on page 58

Eventually leave your snorting friends behind and emerge onto a road. Go straight across, past Rhubarb Cottage, and begin to climb on the wide pathway, passing through wide acres of fields. After 400m the trail reaches a minor road; go straight across and continue uphill. About 600m later cross Lynn Lane. After a little over kilometre the path comes to a further road, which you cross, then continue to climb up a gentle slope.

The path along this section is wide and often used by 4x4s, so do be aware of any approaching vehicles as you meander on; it's easy to lose yourself in the landscape now the roads have been left behind at last. Shortly you'll notice a small copse of trees on the right, known as Nut Wood. Nestled in the greenery is another of the Norfolk Songlines sculptures. The prose here is particularly beautiful, and worth stopping to read 'From Blackwater Carr to Seagate/ Since the plough first broke the bread of land/ Pightles [small enclosure of land] and pieces plots and pastures/To every man his stony acre'.

Once you've fuelled your imagination further, continue along the track, ignoring the public footpath that leads off right as you pass Cockyhoop Cottage and

57

Map continues on page 61

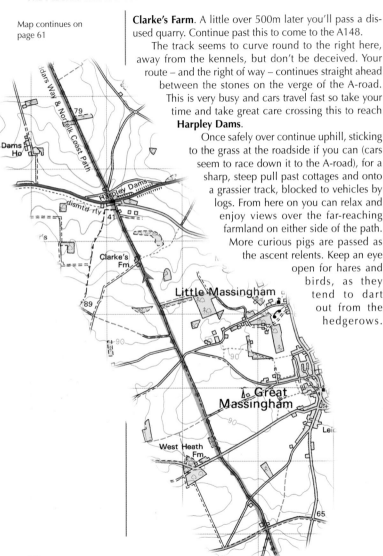

Clarke's Farm. A little over 500m later you'll pass a disused quarry. Continue past this to come to the A148.

The track seems to curve round to the right here, away from the kennels, but don't be deceived. Your route – and the right of way – continues straight ahead between the stones on the verge of the A-road. This is very busy and cars travel fast so take your time and take great care crossing this to reach **Harpley Dams**.

Once safely over continue uphill, sticking to the grass at the roadside if you can (cars seem to race down it to the A-road), for a sharp, steep pull past cottages and onto a grassier track, blocked to vehicles by logs. From here on you can relax and enjoy views over the far-reaching farmland on either side of the path. More curious pigs are passed as the ascent relents. Keep an eye open for hares and birds, as they tend to dart out from the hedgerows.

Note too that the fields are increasingly pockmarked by marl pits.

> As you tread further along the Peddars Way, passing through acres of farmland, you'll notice an increasing number of **marl pits**, relics from our agricultural past. Dating from around 1840–50 these are the remnants of diggings for clay and carbonate of lime – aka marl – which was mixed with manure and used as fertiliser by farmers. They are synonymous with Norfolk and were also dug to provide chalk for composting and clay for brick manufacture. They remain as sloping craters in the landscape, often filled with tangled trees and vegetation. At first they look like landslips, but once identified they will become more obvious and you will spot more and more as you go.

As the path begins to level out keep an eye on the fields to the right to spot some grass-covered bumps. These are Bronze Age tumuli, which have overlooked the route for hundreds of years, even before the Romans used

The fourth of the Norfolk Songlines stones can be found near Nut Wood, Little Massingham

Marl pits – such as this on the path above Harpley Dams – are often seen from the trail

this pathway. The best example is reached just before the road; a sign on the fence gives details of the permissive access that allows you to cross a stile and take a closer look. You are asked not to climb on top of the tumulus to avoid disturbing it.

Nowadays a tumulus appears as nothing more than a grass-covered hillock, but there's much more to it than that. A **tumulus** is a burial mound constructed over a grave, a common practice from around the end of the Neolithic period and into the Bronze Age. The most visible one from the path is estimated to date from the early to middle Bronze Age (1300–1800BC). Its proximity to a number of other tumuli suggests that this area was of great significance at that time.

The Peddars Way continues down to the road where there is a large tree trunk to prevent cars coming down the path. This makes a handy seat for those needing a brief respite or break for lunch.

Cross the road to continue on the path straight ahead. ▶ It is still grassy underfoot and an easy walk between the bracken and hedges from where muntjac deer, foxes and gamebirds often emerge (most likely as startled by you as you will be by them). The track is fairly wide – certainly wide enough for a 4x4 if the tyre tracks are anything to go by – which can make it boggy, particularly after rain.

Take care crossing the minor road after **Amner Minque** and follow the path to a crossroads. Here there is an option (sign-posted) to detour into

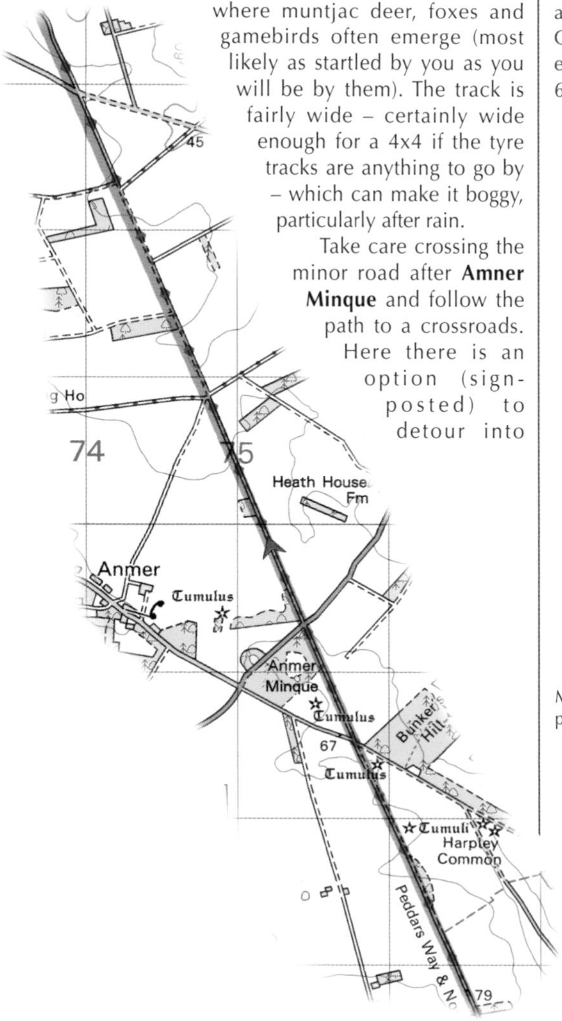

This section is managed by the National Trail office as well as HM The Queen's Sandringham estate which sits 6.5km to the west.

Map continues on page 62

45

g Ho

74   75

Heath House
Fm

Anmer

Tumulus

Anmer
Minque

Tumulus

Bunker
Hill

67

Tumulus

☆ Tumuli
Harpley
Common

Peddars Way & N

79

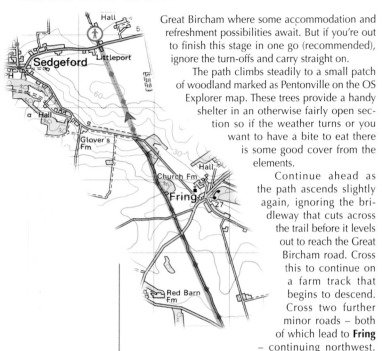

Great Bircham where some accommodation and refreshment possibilities await. But if you're out to finish this stage in one go (recommended), ignore the turn-offs and carry straight on.

The path climbs steadily to a small patch of woodland marked as Pentonville on the OS Explorer map. These trees provide a handy shelter in an otherwise fairly open section so if the weather turns or you want to have a bite to eat there is some good cover from the elements.

Continue ahead as the path ascends slightly again, ignoring the bridleway that cuts across the trail before it levels out to reach the Great Bircham road. Cross this to continue on a farm track that begins to descend. Cross two further minor roads – both of which lead to **Fring** – continuing northwest. The track rises up fairly steeply before finally descending to the actual Fring road where you emerge next to the old ford (on the right).

It is tricky to find on-path accommodation for this stage of the walk, but Sedgeford is a good option as it's not far from the path and offers a couple of overnight choices as well as a pub. It is possible to reach it by turning left onto the road here, but that would miss out a key section of the trail (so is not for purists). Leaving the path here also means taking another road that is far less walker-friendly than the alternative described below.

Carefully cross the road and take the faint, boot-beaten path ahead into the grassy field, and start climbing – for the last time today. Although by no means a big

hill, by this point – with today's distance under your belt – this will start to feel like a real challenge and you'll be relieved when the path levels out at Dovehill Wood. Not far to go now, so start to descend and cut through a gap in the hedge, now with the trees on the right.

A distinctive Bronze Age tumulus sits just off the Peddars Way at Harpley Common

At the corner of the field turn left and follow the path as it funnels you into a narrowing path, heading west. When you can go no further turn right, heading north again, and walk past the line of houses which make up the tiny hamlet of **Littleport**.

The one on-path accommodation option here is at Magazine House – dead ahead across the main road (B1454) – but with only two rooms available this is often booked in advanced. Most walkers – if not continuing onto the next stage immediately – will want to stop in **Sedgeford**. To do this cross the road and turn left, where a pavement leads all the way into the village in under a kilometre – not long in reality but it can feel like an age after the 24km you've already undertaken!

The waymarker at Sedgeford, a good end point for the third stage of the Peddars Way

The Peddars Way follows farm tracks as it heads towards Fring

SEDGEFORD

This small, unassuming village (recorded in the Domesday Book in 1086) is home to one of Norfolk's 124 round-tower churches – St Mary's – that is certainly worth checking out. It is constructed of local flint and has been dated back to the Anglo-Saxon period.

The settlement itself has much earlier origins, backed by archaeological evidence from the Roman, Iron Age and Neolithic periods. Flint tools and gold torcs have been found in gardens here, and it is no coincidence that both the ancient Peddars and Icknield Ways (both of which pre-date the Roman invasion) pass through it.

There are a couple of accommodation options (see the National Trail website, Appendix B) as well as The King William IV Country Inn and Restaurant (which also offers rooms). More local information is available at www.sedgeford.org.uk.

Norfolk Green bus number 402 runs to Hunstanton from the village, but only during school term-time with one service a day at 8.30am. It is an option for those who are planning to do this as a single stage, but it is recommended that if you need to leave the trail here you continue on instead to Holme next the Sea (Stage 4) and get the bus from there, from where the service is much more frequent and convenient. Up-to-date transport options can be found at www.travelinneeastanglia.org.uk.

STAGE 4
Sedgeford to Hunstanton

Start	B1454, Sedgeford (TF 722 368)
Finish	Hunstanton war memorial (TF 672 408)
Distance	12.5km (7¾ miles)
Time	3½hrs
Refreshments	The Gin Trap Inn, Ringstead; The White Horse PH, Holme next the Sea; pubs and cafés in Hunstanton
Toilets	Public toilets at café on Hunstanton promenade, and by golf course at Holme next the Sea
Public transport	Coasthopper bus to King's Lynn and Cromer
Parking	On-street parking and car parks in Hunstanton
Accommodation	B&Bs, hotels and hostels in Hunstanton

Hold your breath – you are about to get your first glimpse of the Norfolk coastline. This stage may be a short day compared to others, but it marks the end of the inland section of the long-distance route. As you pass through the pretty little village of Ringstead you will begin to smell the sea and, at last, feel the soft sand of Holme next the Sea underfoot. A visual feast of all the elements that make up a classic British seaside resort can be enjoyed as you reach Hunstanton and celebrate finishing one half of the National Trail.

Retrace your steps from Sedgeford back to Littleport along the B1454. On reaching the cottages passed at the end on Stage 3 continue straight on the pavement for another few metres, then take the signposted path (National Trail logo) to your left. Sedgeford Magazine will be passed to your right.

Built in the 17th century, the **Magazine Cottage** is something of a local landmark. Magazine buildings are dotted across Britain, and were once used to store gunpowder for either military or engineering work. Chosen for its secure location, rumour has it

Sedgeford Magazine greets walkers on this last stage of the Peddars Way

that there is a secret passageway which runs from Magazine Cottage either to St Mary's Church in the village or out to the coast. Now a private house it is still a very striking building that you cannot help but notice when you start this stage of the trail.

Continue straight on the path, passing the Magazine Farm (and Magazine Wood – a luxury B&B – from where it is said you can watch the sun set over the Norfolk coast due to its elevated position). Here the track becomes grassier and fortunately is closed to any vehicles. Cross the dismantled railway and continue through a field until you come to a wider farm track. Turn left, then a few steps later turn right off it again and into another field. Follow the edge of this, with the hedge to the right, heading northwest towards a line of trees. Walk through a gap in the trees at the field corner, curving left for a few metres before continuing straight on, skirting the trees. It is here that you will get your first glimpse of the sea – a welcome sight after the distance you've put in inland – and it really feels like the Peddars Way portion is coming to a close.

Continue straight on, ignoring the bridleway that branches off right, to begin the descent into **Ringstead**. If you decided not to stop in Sedgeford then Ringstead is a good alternative.

Map continues on page 71

Although a little further on than Sedgeford, the pretty village of **Ringstead** can be a good place to break your journey. It is right on the path and boasts The Gin Trap Inn (offering food and accommodation) as well as The General Store (High Street – open daily, including most Bank Holidays) where you can buy food and drink as well as a whole host of 'hidden treasures'. Ringstead is on the Le Strange estate, owned by the family who also built Sedgeford Magazine in the 17th century. On the official village sign a white line depicted against the backdrop of green fields and country houses represents the long-distance path you are following. For more information about Ringstead see www.ringsteadparish.info.

The path emerges into the village alongside a cluster of houses; note that the road you join is called Peddars Way (South). As you cross over to gain the pavement keep a lookout to the right as cars can quickly swing round from Docking Road. Continue towards the impressive tree ahead then turn left, crossing the road onto the pavement.

Walking into Ringstead, the last village met before reaching the coast

Where the road forks, turn right to continue heading uphill, past the Gin Trap Inn (right) and The General Store, then the war memorial and St Andrew's Church (left). Shortly after this pass the sign for Greater Ringstead. As you reach the village outskirts turn right, passing a line of houses, then take the road on the left – signposted the Peddars Way (North). Cross over onto the right side of the road to follow the pavement.

The old **windmill** at Mill Farm starts to dominate the skyline ahead. This impressive structure was built in 1837–42 and at the time unusually featured six sails to help it turn (in Norfolk most had four). In 1897 the mill ceased operating, and in 1927 was converted to residential use, as it remains today. No sails adorn its great tower now, but you can easily imagine how impressive it would have looked when it was operational.

Once past the row of houses, with the mill on your left, note a public footpath sign pointing off to the right. Do not follow this; instead continue on for a couple more

The windmill at Mill Farm becomes ever-dominant you reach the sea north of Ringstead

The fifth and final Norfolk Songlines sculpture sits above Holme next the Sea where views of the coast entice walkers onwards

steps then cross the road to the left side. Here look out for a well-hidden sign for the National Trail, which cuts through a field to the left, leaving the road behind.

Stay at the top of the field for just under 400m then turn right on a signposted path lined by trees. The sea is getting tantalisingly close now and the sound of the crashing waves can soon be heard. As the path slowly descends you will see the final instalment of the Norfolk Songlines sculptures on your right, a satisfying reminder that the end of the Peddars Way is now is firmly in sight. It bears the inscription 'And I being here have been part of all this/Caught and thrown like sun on water/Have entered into all around me'.

Emerge onto the A149 that links Hunstanton with Holme next the Sea. There is a bus stop here (before you cross the road) if you plan to make a quick getaway into Hunstanton and get transport links home. Otherwise carefully cross the road and follow the lane north, heading for the sea. Cars do come down this so stay alert. Ignore the road that turns off right, continuing straight on as the road bends slightly left past the caravan park. If you have an older map you may think that's you've missed the path; until 2008 it ran along the inland side of the golf course next to the River Hun. Now, however, it rather more pleasantly runs along the coast proper, so continue straight ahead.

Map continues on page 74

There are toilets on the left as you approach the golf course. A few steps later, after dodging the golf balls (something of a minor hazard on this section), the track becomes sandy underfoot and you reach the crossroads and signpost that designate the official end of the Peddars Way – congratulations!

Reaching the sea – as it would have been for the Romans, and before them the Iceni (who trod this path for necessity rather than pleasure) – is a significant point on the Peddars Way. Holme next the Sea is where HRH Prince Charles officially opened the whole route in 1986.

The sand dunes between Holme and Old Hunstanton offer great views down the coast

HOLME NEXT THE SEA

For accommodation away from the brash beachside resort of Hunstanton – or as a base from which to start or finish the Peddars Way section of the path – Holme is certainly a good option. There are several self-catering establishments as well as B&Bs and a pub, The White Horse. If staying here for a few days – aside from the obvious exploration of the nearby sand dunes – St Mary's Church is worth a look.

This village also has a real claim to fame as it was on the beach at Holme where Seahenge was discovered. Dated to 2050BC, this Bronze Age monument consisted of a felled giant oak tree buried in the sand with its roots sticking upwards, surrounded by 56 posts cut from smaller oaks. It is thought to have been used as an altar or ceremonial site. It was reclaimed by the sea and forgotten until 1998 when the receding tide revealed it once more. Rising water levels meant it would soon have been lost to Mother Nature once more, so a fairly controversial decision – amid protests from Druid and pagan groups – was made by English Heritage to dig it up and display it in Flag Fen in Peterborough, where it remains. Although it can no longer be seen at Holme, you can certainly enjoy standing on the wide expanse of dunes and imagining its grand structure amid the silt. For more information on Holme see www.holme-next-the-sea.co.uk.

Now you must decide – if you haven't already – whether to walk the National Trail in its entirety, or miss out the 8km there-and-back into Hunstanton and start the coastal section by walking northeast here at Holme. If you do want to do it all, but don't relish the thought of repeating a section, get the bus from Holme to Hunstanton and start walking from there (see Stage 5). However, the walk along the coast into Hunstanton is by no means unpleasant or difficult, so a stroll from here along the sea is a good option (and well worth a repeat in the opposite direction).

To reach Hunstanton turn left at the crossroads and follow the path as it weaves up and over the sand dunes. In good weather the views over to the cliffs, the white lighthouse and out to sea are pretty spectacular, so keep your camera ready. Skirt the upper edges of the golf course as you pass a number of pretty beachside houses on the way to **Old Hunstanton**. Here turn left to emerge in front of the RNLI lifeboat station then turn right in front of it, taking the once again sandy track behind the beach huts. Follow this, passing the car park to the left, and more huts to the right, to reach another car park at **St Edmunds Point**. Follow the path alongside this, heading towards the lighthouse.

Pass a cage that held the beacon that was lit here on 19 July 1988, along with 400 others around the country, to mark the 400th anniversary of the sighting of the Spanish Armada in 1588. Continue below it and along the grassy promenade to reach the lighthouse. Built in 1665 and fired by wood and coal, then rebuilt in its current form in 1840, it sadly ceased operation in 1922 and is now impressive holiday accommodation. A few steps from it are the remains of St Edmund's Chapel.

St Edmund's Chapel was erected in 1272 in memory of St Edmund, a man who landed in Hunstanton in AD855 and was crowned King of East Anglia. He led a battle against the invading Vikings but was captured and then martyred, becoming one of the

The unmistakeable striped cliffs of Hunstanton glisten in the sunset

first English patron saints. Although there is little left of this building you can see the traditional flint construction and a manicured garden makes this a pleasant place to sit for a well-earned rest. It is also a great spot to get a photo of the lighthouse, which you can frame within a still extant archway. The site is now Grade II listed.

The remains of St Edmund's Chapel on the National Trail as it nears Hunstanton

From here, as you edge closer into the town centre, the route shown on OS maps heads along the road, but in reality the waymarked track (and recommended option)

sticks close to the cliff top, away from the vehicles. At the café bear right with the path as it curves round the buildings and follow it straight on (not descending to the beach) through the gardens. Pass the war memorial with its bright poppies before climbing up to join the road. Here a simple sign marks the true start of the Norfolk Coast Path, stating that you have 76km (47 miles) to go before you reach Cromer and the end of the National Trail.

Those heading home now can carry on to the bus station to catch the Coasthopper bus to King's Lynn or Cromer for rail links with the national rail network (see below).

HUNSTANTON

Hunstanton is a great place to start the Norfolk Coast Path section of this National Trail as well as an ideal base to rest and recharge for those who've just walked the Peddars Way. It is also a fantastic place to spend a summer's evening in traditional British holiday fashion: with a pot of jellied eels or some fish and chips from one of the seaside crab stands or kiosks, enjoying an ice-cream, playing on the amusements at the pierside arcades, taking a boat trip out on The Wash, scaring yourself silly on one of the fairground rides or simply taking a stroll by the sea. For those who just want to rest, there's always the option of hiring a stripy deckchair and chilling out as you watch the world go by and the tide come in. This is Victorian seaside fun at its best, and there really can be no better way to while away the evening.

There are many different accommodation choices, ranging from hostels to hotels (see Appendix B). If these are full – and they do get busy in the summer – try Old Hunstanton, further down the path (more details on www. west-norfolk.gov.uk). There is also an abundance of restaurants to choose from – whether you fancy a sit-down evening meal, a spot of gluttony in a greasy spoon café or a bag of chips from the takeaway – you certainly won't go hungry here.

Transport links are superb; this is the start/finish point of the regular Coasthopper bus (see Stage 5) that runs to the end of the National Trail at Cromer. There are also regular and reliable bus links to King's Lynn which marry up with train departures onwards towards Ely, London and beyond (for buses go to www.travelineeastanglia.co.uk; for trains www.nationalrail.co.uk).

STAGE 5

Hunstanton to Burnham Deepdale

Start	Hunstanton war memorial (TF 672 408)
Finish	Burnham Deepdale (TF 803 443)
Distance	19.25km (12 miles)
Time	5½hrs
Refreshments	The Orange Tree PH, Thornham; The Ship PH, Brancaster; Deepdale Café, Burnham Deepdale
Toilets	Hunstanton Promenade
Public transport	Coasthopper bus at most villages on route
Parking	Limited on-street parking in Burnham Deepdale
Accommodation	B&Bs, pubs, hostel and camping in Burnham Deepdale; also options in Old Hunstanton, Thornham and Brancaster

Leave behind the hustle and bustle of Hunstanton – the official start of the Norfolk Coast Path – to explore a wilder side of the coastline. The famous striped cliffs and pretty beach houses in Old Hunstanton give way to the expansive sand dunes and silt banks of Holme next the Sea. Enjoy the amazing array of migrating and sea-dwelling birds before heading inland for a brief section that will remind you of the Peddars Way. Edge behind the old Roman fort at Brancaster then walk the final few steps past the small harbour and into the hamlet of Burnham Deepdale.

Approximately 76km (47 miles) lie between Hunstanton and Cromer – but what wonderful miles they are! From sea to saltmarsh, cliff to shingle, with a smattering of quirky villages and bird reserves in between – this is one section of walking you won't want to end.

The path (and Stage 5 of the complete route) officially begins by the war memorial opposite the main town green, indicated by a marker post. Continue past the giant painted poppies at the cross, past the patches of grass and along to the café. Here (as at the end of Stage 4) there is a choice of routes. You can retrace your steps

TRANSPORT LINKS ON THE NORFOLK COAST PATH

Compared to the Peddars Way section the Norfolk Coast Path is a dream for anyone wanting to complete, or tackle it as a series of single days, utilising public transport. Running between Hunstanton and Cromer is the excellent Coasthopper bus service, operated by Norfolk Green. This is reliable and very frequent with services more or less hourly in winter (until around 4–5pm) and half hourly in the summer (until approximately 6pm). It is so efficient that most locals use it too! Single and return tickets are available, as well as one-, two- and three-day tickets, meaning that you can plan where to stay at different places along the path each night in advance; or choose to base yourself at one village along the route and take the bus each day to your next start point, catching it back again at the end of the day from one of the many bus stops along the way.

But the fantastic public transport options don't end there. From Hunstanton you can get a bus to King's Lynn station (onward connections available to Ely – connections on to Peterborough and beyond – as well as London); and from Cromer buses run to Norwich or even Yarmouth. For up-to-date routes, timetables and ticket prices, check out www.coasthopper.co.uk.

along the coast to Holme next the Sea, passing the café and walking along the grassy esplanade to the lighthouse and remains of St Edmund's Chapel (see Stage 4). The recommended option, however, is to vary your route and check out Hunstanton's famous striped cliffs up close and personal. ▸

For the beach option, instead of continuing straight on to pass the café take the path left which zigzags down to the lower promenade, level with the beach. Here turn right to access the sand. Navigation is a doddle as you just walk straight on, keeping the cliffs to your right and sea to your left. Watch your step as you go, as there are many slippery seaweed-covered rocks and you are likely to be distracted by the dazzling colours of the cliffs above.

As you pass below **St Edmund's Point**, nearly level with the lighthouse, look out for the wreck of the Sheraton, a trawler built in 1907. In 1947, after her working life was over she was moored up on The Wash ready

Remember to check the tides before you take to the beach (see Appendix B) so that you don't get cut off by the sea; at times of high tide this beach route is impassable.

The official start of the Norfolk Coast Path in Hunstanton on a chilly day

to be used as a target ship, but broke her line and washed up here. Now all that remains of her hull lies close to the cliffs for all to investigate.

Hunstanton Cliffs are renowned for their striped layers – literally thrusting their geological make-up at you, whether or not you are interested! Bands of brown carstone – sand cemented together by iron oxide (aka rust) – white chalk and red limestone make these crumbling rocky giants visually distinctive from others in the UK.

Huge sections of cliff face regularly crack off and fall onto the sand below, so keep a safe distance. However, watch out for the smaller offcuts – in particular the chalky ones – as these lay under the sea over 70 million years ago and are a hotbed for fossils. Look closely and you may see the remains of plants, cuttlefish, sea urchins or even shark's teeth.

Once the cliffs come to an end, you'll see the path leading up to the car park on the right. Take this, but just before you reach the top swing left to re-join the National Trail behind the start of the wooden beach huts.

Continue on the pathway behind the huts as it undulates like the waves to emerge in **Old Hunstanton** by the RNLI boat shed. Cross in front of this to join the path that again continues behind the huts. Skirt the edge of the golf club at first before turning up left to reach the top of the sand dunes. Follow the path along here, long grass tracing it either side, until it returns you to the corner of the fenceline with the golf course. Here the path curves round to the right. Follow it, ignoring the path that leads down to the sea, to reach the crossroads with the Peddars Way which stretches off south to Knettishall Heath (see Stages 1–4).

Carry straight ahead on the sandy path. You will pass small ponds and meander through swathes of buckthorn and electric purple sea lavender on your way to **Gore Point**. Here you'll see a sign advising of the dangers of exploring the beach beyond the dunes. The tides often reshape the sands here and you can quickly find yourself stranded without much warning, so any off-piste exploration you are tempted to undertake needs due care and attention.

Continue on the path, ignoring this alluring deviation. A handy wooden boardwalk traverses the tops of the dunes, before veering to the

Map continues on page 80

79

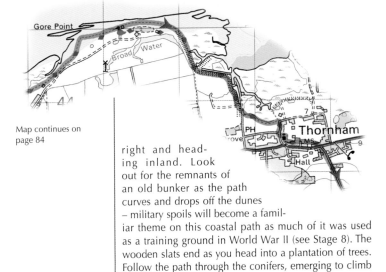

Map continues on
page 84

right and head-
ing inland. Look
out for the remnants of
an old bunker as the path
curves and drops off the dunes
– military spoils will become a famil-
iar theme on this coastal path as much of it was used
as a training ground in World War II (see Stage 8). The
wooden slats end as you head into a plantation of trees.
Follow the path through the conifers, emerging to climb
steps on the right up to the edge of **Broad Water**, part of
the Holme Bird Observatory and Nature Reserve.

Established in 1962, **Holme Bird Observatory and
Nature Reserve** was sited due to its strategic position on avian migration routes. From here birds
arriving, leaving and passing through Norfolk could
be observed and recorded by wardens. Since opening, over 50,000 birds have been ringed (for identi-
fication) and 300-plus species recorded.

As well as birds, the habitat attracts moths, but-
terflies and dragonflies. Visitors have a choice of
five hides, each overlooking a different habitat or
feeding station – including a sea-watching one, said
to be the first in Norfolk.

If you fancy nipping in from the path, you can
do so via a gate. On entry – unless you are a mem-
ber – you will need to find the warden to buy a
single-day permit (closed on Mondays). For more

information see www.norfolkwildlifetrust.co.uk and click on Nature Reserves.

The path is now on a sea defence bank, which can get fairly waterlogged and muddy – particularly after rain. Here you'll likely see some wading birds probing in the mud. Continue to follow the path as it heads away from the sea, bearing in a southerly direction. You'll walk adjacent to a car park, popular with birdwatchers. Notice here the number of boats that are stranded on the mud, adding to the feeling of wilderness.

Continue past this and start to walk parallel to and above a minor road. Follow it until the path cuts down to the tarmac, then cross over to turn left onto the National Trail, which is signposted. Immediately to the right are the remains of an old windmill – if you can make it out through the reeds! Carry on along the path to cross a bridge, and immediately afterwards turn right again to join the road into **Thornham**.

Hunstanton's lighthouse stands tall en route to Old Hunstanton

Look out for the birds – fulmars in particular – that nest in the vegetation above Hunstanton's cliffs

Follow the road into the village, passing the church on your left and The Orange Tree pub on your right (a recommended eatery), to emerge onto the A149. There is a Coasthopper bus stop here as well as plenty of accommodation options (see www.thornham-norfolk.co.uk for more information). Otherwise turn left onto the main road and follow the pavement until you reach a road on the right signposted to Choseley.

Snow transforms the sand dunes on the way to Old Hunstanton

Turn right and follow the road, now uphill, heading inland. It feels a little odd to be walking southeast, clearly away from the seafront on what is a coastal path; but there is no safe way to continue along the coastal marshes between Thornham and Brancaster. ▶ As this is a minor but fast and fairly busy road, be careful and walk on the verge whenever practical.

The road is virtually poker straight with few turn-offs, and if you knuckle down it's not long before it begins to sweep left. As it does, before you reach **Choseley**, there's a small patch of trees where the route is waymarked left; follow the path through the woods, emerging into a field.

This 2km climb alongside the road will make you appreciate the sea views all the more when you regain them.

Keeping the hedgeline to your left follow the path through the field. Cross the first minor road and go straight on past farm buildings. The track can be pretty torn up by agricultural traffic, so be wary of the depths of any puddles!

Soon another minor road (Chalkpit Road) is reached. Cross this and continue heading northeast until, approximately 600m later, the path turns sharp left. Follow it downhill, due north. After School Farm the track bends right then left again, eventually reaching some houses. Continue past these, still heading downhill; the path bends right to deposit you

at a crossroads of the A149 and B1153 in **Brancaster** village.

Cross the main A-road heading north (signposted 'Access to the Beach'), passing St Mary's Church on your right. At the National Trust sign turn right off the road to skirt the houses on the edge of Brancaster with the saltmarsh stretching out to The Wash on your left. This quaint little village is another option for accommodation (The Ship pub and hotel is highly recommended) and a Coasthopper bus stop. Along here the path mainly follows a raised wooden boardwalk over boggy ground, a much easier prospect. Cross the stile and continue straight on, heading east to pass behind houses and alongside the Roman fort of Branodunum.

First excavated in 1846, and built in the AD230s, the name of this **Roman fort** is said to derive from the Celtic language, meaning 'fort of Bran'. It was part of the Saxon Shore military defences along with a series of other garrison forts constructed along the coast.

The combination of sand, snow and sea make the Norfolk Coast Path particularly spectacular in winter

A dusk walk from Choseley sees the Norfolk Coast Path take an inland turn on the way to Brancaster

In Roman times its northern edge would have sat right against the sea forming something of a harbour, but since the shoreline has receded it now sits inland. Evidence has been found of a civilian settlement on its eastern and western sides, dating back to the second or even first centuries. It is believed that before the Roman fort was constructed, a wooden fort would have stood in its place around the time of the revolt of Boudicca and the Iceni. However, any remains of the civilian quarters are thought to have been built over in the 1970s when Brancaster was developed.

Only earthworks remain on this once-grand fort, so you have to use your imagination to picture how it might have looked. Entry is free.

Soon you will emerge through a gate. Turn left to pass behind some houses into the Staithe Yacht Club and working harbour which resembles something of a boat graveyard, with parts of cabins and hulls strewn across the place. Here it can be difficult to see where the path goes but, with the water in front of you, look to your right and you'll see it weave between two fisherman's sheds. From here an obvious track heads east, behind the long gardens of some houses.

About a kilometre later the path reaches a cross-roads; one leads out to sea, one continues east and the other heads inland. Turn right to head inland, passing under the trees. Go straight on to join the road that leads into **Burnham Deepdale**. Carry on along it to reach the A149. Across the road is the Dalegate marketplace where you can pick up food supplies; you can find accommodation in the campsite or hostel, or catch the Coasthopper bus.

BURNHAM DEEPDALE

Of all the villages on the Norfolk Coast Path this has to be the best if you're trying to walk this long-distance route on a budget. Here you'll find Deepdale Backpackers, which offers camping, hostel or yurt accommodation to walkers – depending on your budget.

Next door is a garage with a handy store where you can not only buy snacks and sandwiches to take on your walk, but also toiletries and general groceries.

If some retail therapy is what you're after, there is also a clothes shop on offer. But if you're staying overnight the pièce de résistance is the Deepdale Café – a kind of upmarket greasy spoon that welcomes walkers with big cups of tea and hearty breakfasts as well as large slabs of cake to take away (bear in mind that it closes at 4pm on most days).

For information on Burnham Deepdale and nearby Brancaster Staithe see Appendix B and www.brancasterstaithe.co.uk.

STAGE 6
Burnham Deepdale to Stiffkey

Start	Burnham Deepdale (TF 803 443)
Finish	Stiffkey General Store (TF 969 431)
Distance	23km (14¼ miles)
Time	6½hrs
Refreshments	The Hero PH, Burnham Overy Staithe; Holkham Hall Tearooms, Holkham; pubs and cafés in Wells-next-the-Sea and Stiffkey
Toilets	Wells-next-the-Sea
Public transport	Coasthopper bus at Stiffkey, and most villages on route
Parking	Very limited parking in Stiffkey
Accommodation	Pub B&B and self-catering options in Stiffkey

The cries of seabirds and the sound of crashing waves accompany this stage of the Coast Path along the ragged land that fringes the sea. The occasional stretch inland leads past old windmills, military bunkers and their associated roads that now go nowhere. The windy but gloriously expansive Holkham Beach gives way to the busy harbour town of Wells-next-the-Sea, where the tangy scent of salt and vinegar from the fish and chip shops will tempt you to stop; but carry on a little further through the once more remote saltmarshes to finish in the peaceful village of Stiffkey.

From **Burnham Deepdale** cross the A419 and walk up the small road opposite the garage, towards the sea, with the church on your right and continue straight on under trees on a loose, stony track to re-join the National Trail. Now on it, turn right and then left to follow it to the sea, sweeping round **Deepdale Marsh** to the right with **Scolt Head Island National Nature Reserve** to the left.

Ever since 1923 this section of coast has been under protection due to its importance as a **breeding ground for birds**. The mix of sand dunes, marshland

and rocky shingle make it something of a mecca for different species of seabird, including oystercatchers and ringed plovers. Come here most days – any time of the year – and you are guaranteed to spot birdwatchers with their binoculars firmly fixed on the island. The OS map shows at least one path leading out to Scolt Head and along the coast, and on the ground you will spot some well-trodden routes. However, owing to the dangers of rising water and ankle-sucking saltmarsh, it is strongly advised that you do not follow in their footsteps. Instead you can take a boat from Burnham Overy Staithe to visit the Nature Reserve. Natural England currently maintain the area and more information about its plants and wildlife can be found at www. naturalengland.org.uk.

You'll be walking on a raised grassy seabank, which can be fairly muddy underfoot. The sounds of the birds will undoubtedly increase as you go, punctuated by the crashing waves and (usually) whipping wind.

Approaching the windmill on the outskirts of Burnham Overy Staithe

Continue on the path as it heads east before swinging right, first bearing southeast, then southwest back inland. The windmill (once a working mill but now holiday accommodation) on the outskirts of Burnham Overy Staithe will start to dominate the view ahead. After just over a kilometre you'll come to a T-junction. Turn left onto the waymarked National Trail, over the River Burn, and walk diagonally through the field. This will take you to the hedgeline running parallel to the A149. Here turn left to skirt the top of the field, keeping to the field side of the hedge until it funnels you out onto the roadside. Keep following the road and shortly you'll reach the village of **Burnham Overy Staithe** where you turn left, following the acorn symbols down the street and round to the right to reach the small quay, packed with boats. There isn't much in the way of accommodation here – except for the windmill (www.nationaltrustcottages. co.uk) – but there is The Hero pub for refreshment (www. theheroburnhamovery.co.uk).

Turn left onto the raised grassy bank that, similar to the last section of path to Scolt Head, sweeps out towards the sea once more. You'll be edging the brown sand of Overy Creek, heading ever closer to the golden sand dunes. As the path begins to forge due east ignore the footpath that

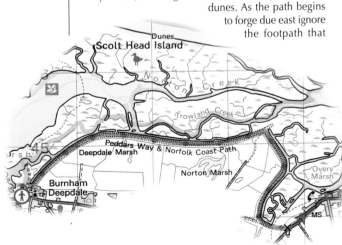

comes in from the south and instead turn left to head out to sea. Soon the path crosses a wooden boardwalk, which makes for much easier progress. Continue to follow this to the top of the sand dunes overlooking the sea, with the beach stretching out in both directions.

Horse riders make use of the bridleway on the Norfolk Coast Path between Brancaster and Holkham

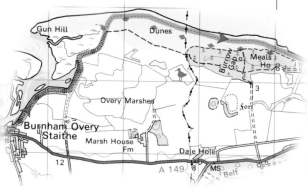

Map continues on page 94

Though the path appears to direct you along the tops of the dunes to your right this is hard going and the dunes are fragile so instead, if tides allow, make your way down to the beach and turn right, keeping the sea to your left. You now have a true coastal walk along to Holkham Gap (approximately 3km away). Navigation is easy, leaving you free to enjoy the sounds of the waves lapping against the shore as you notice the undoubtedly increasing number of people on the beach. From horse riders, birdwatchers and long-distance-path backpackers to casual day walkers and even sunbathers (there's a discreetly placed nudist beach about halfway along if you're in touch with your inner exhibitionist) it seems the whole world and his dog come here to enjoy the scenery.

HOLKHAM

Picturesque Holkham Bay is thought to have been the location of a failed revolt by the native Iceni tribe against the Romans in AD47. The remains of a fort are marked on the OS map near Bone's Drive, which matches closely the description of this rebellion in Roman historian Tacitus's log, written in 109BC. Today the mood is anything but warlike: those enjoying the tree-lined and beach-side walking will be far too contented to have any thoughts of an uprising! Boardwalks lead the way through the sand to bird hides from where you are invited to while away your time watching our feathered friends swoop and dive in the woodland (and also get a good view of the old fort). There's a car park (charge) at Lady Ann's Drive, the leafy boulevard just off the A149 coast road, from where the coast path can be accessed. However, it fills up very quickly, especially in the summer.

Across the road, beyond the houses of the village of Holkham, sits the imposing Holkham Hall and estate. In the late 18th and early 19th centuries this was the home of the agricultural reformer Thomas Coke (pronounced 'Cook'). He used his land to graze cattle, sheep and pigs, and for growing crops. Now his home and estate is a huge draw for tourists and that, along with this stretch of coastline, sees thousands of visitors every year. As well as the hall visitors can check out a museum, pottery centre, deer park and tearooms. For more information about the estate's opening times see www. holkhamhall.co.uk.

If there are no waymarkers you can add your own on Holkham Beach

As you progress further along the path, woodland begins to appear to your right, home to many birdwatching hides. The trees are a mix of pine and scrub, strategically planted in 1860 to offer protection from the wind-blown sand to the village of **Holkham,** itself sited on land reclaimed from the sea. As well as a number of birds it is also home to other wildlife including the rare natterjack toad. Stick close to the edge of the woodland as it curves round to the right towards the cleave of **Holkham Gap**. There's a handy bench here, a great place to stop for a breather as it offers one of the best vistas over the beach and out to sea.

Once you've had your fill of the views, climb the steps up to the wooden boardwalk and follow it south,

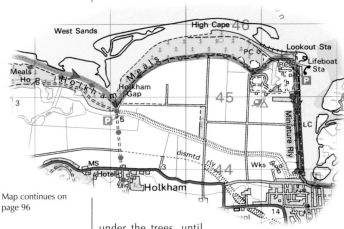

Map continues on
page 96

under the trees, until
you see the vehicles in
the car park on Lady Anne's Drive looming ahead.
Just as you get close, as the boardwalk ends, turn sharp
left onto the waymarked path, once again heading in an
easterly direction.

Here you are now sheltered from the coast by the
woodland. Sea views locked away temporarily, the path
provides easy walking, flanked by fields on one side and

*The seafront at Wells-
next-the-Sea is home
to an array of brightly
coloured beach huts*

trees on the other. You will probably pass several tele-scope-carrying twitchers who regularly head here. The path continues to hug the trees, curving round to the right, then left to pass a boating lake; note the caravans in the nearby holiday park. Brace yourself as the peace and quiet of Holkham is about to come to a halt as you near the seaside resort of **Wells-next-the-Sea**.

Continue straight on to emerge into a large car park with public toilets and a café. The path passes in front of the eatery and climbs up to the walkway then turns right to head into the hustle and bustle of the seaside town. Before heading onto The Bank it's a worthwhile two-minute detour to check out the beach again by heading left – if only to see the way it has morphed from the wild expansive dunes you walked past earlier to a quaint, but busy, tourist beach. Here you'll see rows of decorated beach huts and golden sands stretching out from the trees. It's an idyllic spot and in summer has the crowds to prove it. ▶

One of the small beach huts here will set you back tens of thousands of pounds – a small price to pay for such a trendy coastal postcode, perhaps...

WELLS-NEXT-THE-SEA

Once a major port between King's Lynn and Yarmouth, this seaside town was hit hard when the railway arrived in 1857, rendering transport by sea second choice. Now it is home to leisure cruisers and day-tripping boaters rather than the hardened sea dogs of years gone by transporting important cargo along the coast.

Today the town is known more for its tourist attractions than trade status and as such has managed to survive as a summer destination. Here there are a number of accommodation options – from B&Bs to pubs and a YHA hostel – making this an easy place to either stop en route while walking the whole National Trail, or as a base from which to walk it using the Coasthopper buses. There is an array of places to eat too. For more information on Wells see www.wells-guide.co.uk.

For those with more time to sightsee, just outside the town is the Wells and Walsingham Light Railway, the longest 10¼in gauge steam railway in the world. A return trip will see you enjoying a 13km journey on the old Great Eastern Railway track to Walshingham. For train times and up-to-date prices see www.wellswalsinghamrailway.co.uk.

When you've had your fill of the beach, head inland alongside the miniature railway down to the harbour. Here turn left, keeping on the harbourside. Here you can peer down at the boats docked below, including a moored-up seafood restaurant often identified by the swarms of seagulls that flock overhead. On the other side of the road are a number of chippies and greasy spoon cafés. Whatever your choice of refreshment it is an appealing place to spend time, pick up a souvenir or watch the gulls hover. But you still have some distance to cover, so to finish Stage 6 continue past the chandlery and slipway keeping to the left when the road forks, then keep left again to climb up onto the bank behind the boatyard. Here the constant clank of bells, fixed to the masts of the boats to deter seagulls, echoes through the air.

This can be a particularly muddy section of the path and you certainly wouldn't want to slip off into the patchwork of saltmarsh that drops down to the left, so take your time. Suddenly the sounds of the shops and arcades seem a million miles away as all buildings disappear, with nothing but wild marshland expanding out to sea to provide entertainment.

Follow the bank as it turns right to temporarily head inland, then left again heading east, before descending to the left again, once more heading north towards the sea. You'll be walking through some trees for a short while before

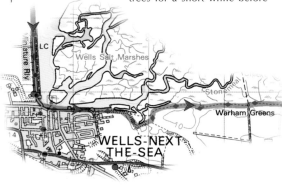

The boats tie up at the harbour town of Wells-next-the-Sea while the seagulls fly above

At times this stretch seems more like the tracks on the Peddars Way, with wide expanses of countryside leading off right and the sea feeling very far away.

the path emerges into open fields and curves to the right, heading east once more.

Though on the map the distance to Stiffkey doesn't seem that much, with the inevitable wind bringing with it a chill from the sea, as well as the often water-logged track underfoot, this section can feel like quite a challenge. ◄ You may notice several paths stretching out onto the network of marshland to the left, and perhaps some people exploring them, but a safer and more eco-friendly route (the marsh is fragile) is to be had by sticking to the path.

Soon evidence of this area's former military use becomes apparent. Concrete roads suddenly appear and lead off to dead ends, and metal tracks protrude from the mud, seeming very out of place. This area formed part of a very important training ground for the armed forces in both World Wars (see Stage 8).

Ignore any roads that, although appearing to offer an easier route, deviate from the main trail. Although the going is tough you finally reach a car park at Green Way. Here a sign points inland to **Stiffkey**. Ignore this – it may be the shortest distance to the road, but by taking the next

Crab baskets on the quay at Wells-next-the-Sea

turn-off you'll be in a better position to re-join the path at the start of Stage 7 and come out near the cakes and coffee on offer in the general store! So carry straight on, still heading east, past the parked cars and shortly, just after a disused bunker, you'll see another signpost pointing to a public footpath that heads inland. Turn right to climb the short but steep slope to emerge onto a farmer's field. This is Hollow Lane.

Follow the path past the houses and along the now much wider track. Pass a grand house on the right and a playground and public playing field on the left, before descending a gravel drive onto the main road (A149). Turn left here, taking care along the road, and cross over to the post office where you'll find refreshments and the bus stop for the Coasthopper.

STIFFKEY

Despite being a small little village, Stiffkey has a couple of local celebrities to its name. During World War II it was home to the author Henry Williamson, who wrote *Tarka the Otter* as well as the lesser-known *The Story of Norfolk Farm*. Perhaps more notorious, however, was its other former resident, the Rev Harold Davidson, who in the thirties – due to his penchant for visiting certain establishments in Soho – became known as the 'Prostitutes Padre'. He vehemently denied this and sought, unsuccessfully, to clear his name. He then went to Blackpool, using his notoriety to appear in music hall and, later, in a lion's cage as part of an act in Skegness. Unfortunately during the latter he met a grisly end – courtesy of the lion – and his scandalous reputation became legend in these parts.

Scandal aside this place also used to be famous for its particular variety of cockles, known as Stewkey Blues ('Stewkey' is thought to be in reference to the marshy valley where the village sits), which have a dark blue/grey shell. Though quite the delicacy centuries ago this industry sadly declined and now the main talking point food-wise is the homemade cakes on sale in the general store and post office behind the Coasthopper bus stop.

Among its decorative flint houses are a couple of overnight options, including the Red Lion pub as well as some self-catering cottages. For current availability check www.glavenvalley.co.uk or the National Trail website (see Appendix B).

STAGE 7
Stiffkey to Cley next the Sea

Start	Stiffkey General Store (TF 969 431)
Finish	Coast Road, Cley next the Sea (TG 044 437)
Distance	11km (6¾ miles)
Time	3½hrs
Refreshments	Blakeney Hotel and The White Horse PH, Blakeney; pubs and cafés in Cley next the Sea
Toilets	Blakeney Harbour and Morston
Public transport	Coasthopper bus in Stiffkey, Blakeney and Cley next the Sea
Parking	Public car park in Cley next the Sea
Accommodation	B&Bs in Cley next the Sea

Hardy walkers may be tempted to tack this section onto another to make an epic day, but the delightful villages of Stiffkey, Morston and Blakeney deserve more than a passing glance. Indulge yourself and take the time to gaze out towards Blakeney Point and see if you can make out the depression left behind by the chapel that once sat on its banks. End the day with a stroll in the proud windmill town of Cley next the Sea, in preparation for the final stage of the trail.

To access the coastal path from **Stiffkey** take the narrow gravel drive heading north, a few steps west of and opposite the post office and general store (a good place to get snacks and drinks for your walk). Head north past the playing field (on the right) and the houses (left). Pass a home complete with a bunker-type building, keep going towards the trees and through the gap to cross a public footpath running west–east, and descend the short but steep slope to a wider track. Turn right to rejoin the Norfolk Coast Path.

Head east as the path, once more, skirts the edge of the saltmarsh. It is fairly wide at this point but can get waterlogged, so look for stony patches to avoid the

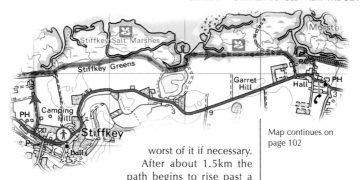

Map continues on
page 102

worst of it if necessary. After about 1.5km the path begins to rise past a picturesque lake to the right – often busy with geese and ducks – and the outflow of Freshes Creek to the left. You will start to spy moored sailboats bobbing on the water as you pass this section, before swinging round left, heading towards the coast once more. Continue on as the sights and smells of the sea begin to play on your senses. In approximately 50m turn right, heading east again, once more passing rows of small boats.

Follow the waymarked path as it curves through bushes, heading roughly east. In about half a kilometre comes a section where the ground is often so saturated that crossing it is not recommended. Luckily a gap in the fence on the right allows you to take a detour via a farm track, which returns to the path a few metres later, through another fence gap.

Continue along the track to suddenly find yourself in **Morston**, once more surrounded by birdwatchers and dog walkers. Follow the path as it curves round to head briefly south into a lane. Here you turn left to climb some steps and then bear east to walk among boats stored on hard standing, now heading towards the National Trust Centre where you'll find toilets and a snack kiosk.

Although **Morston** is only a tiny hamlet – and one that, due to its secluded location, cannot be seen until you reach it – in high summer this area can be

Boats line the marshes at Freshes Creek en route to Morston

very busy. There is a small campsite just before you turn left to reach the National Trust Centre, a possible base for the coastal section of the National Trail, and The Anchor Inn is found in the village. If you continue down the small lane you will reach the main road and the Coasthopper bus. If you are charmed by the place and want to linger here a little longer, boat trips to Blakeney Point run from the small quay. For more walking options inland head to

Morston Downs where a path leads to Wiveton Downs, a Site of Specific Scientific Interest (SSSI) on account of geological evidence of the effects of the last Ice Age. For accommodation options see www. glavenvalley.co.uk or the National Trail website (see Appendix B).

The path climbs up left onto the seabank. Once on it turn right and begin your journey towards Blakeney. Underfoot the track is good at first but can get slippery and churned up after rain – particularly where another path joins by Morston Downs. Continue onwards as the path begins to sweep right towards the town, keeping its distance from it for the time being as you trace the edge of **Agar Creek** and pass fields of ponies. You eventually emerge into **Blakeney** by the quayside.

Turn right to reach the town sign (a general store can be found up the road directly in front of you), then turn left to walk alongside docked boats into the National Trust car park.

BLAKENEY

The town has a longstanding relationship with the sea. Historically it was not only a significant seaport but also an important base for ships. When the Spanish Armada threatened to invade in 1588, some of the ships mustered to defend the country came from this unassuming port town. As you walk through its quaint, cobbled streets look out for the signs on the town hall that mark the flood levels at different times. Although the sea has benefited the community, it has also been its biggest threat, and from time to time flood warnings are still issued. Sadly since the early 20th century the harbour has silted up and now only small tourist boats can make their way up its channel and out to sea; this is another place that becomes very busy in summertime.

Good places to try the locally-caught seafood are the characterful Blakeney Hotel or The White Horse. There are public toilets next to the National Trust car park at the seafront. If you want to use this as an access point to the coast path there is a handy free car park just off the B1156 (on your right if approaching from the coast road), just behind the Coasthopper bus stop. For more information on Blakeney see www.blakeneyonline.co.uk.

The seaside town of Blakeney offers food, refreshment and a friendly welcome to walkers

This section can be particularly prone to a strong and icy wind.

To continue on the path cross the car park, climb the seabank ahead and turn left. Follow it as it heads towards the sea, in a northerly direction. ▶ You will start to catch your first glimpse of Blakeney Point. Where the path begins to curve east once more it feels really wild and a long way from Blakeney, despite being just a kilometre away. Littering the sides of the tracks are boats that have seen better days, their rotting hulls contorted and twisted as they lie decaying on the marsh. You will spot well-trodden paths heading out onto the marsh and over the creeks, but these are not safe and anyone following one of can easily be cut off from the mainland. Stay on the bank the whole way; do not be tempted by the left path at the fork towards Blakeney Point, but keep right.

Those who have read Robert MacFarlane's book *The Wild Places* will know of his mission to overnight on **Blakeney Point**, a 4.8km shingle spit, as part of his quest to discover wilderness in the UK. While a camp on such a dicey point – that does regularly get cut off from the mainland – is certainly best reserved for those who know what they are doing, it is easy to see why he did it. Its windswept location offers an 'ends of the earth' experience, and the combination of saltmarsh, vegetated shingle and sand dune attracts a variety of wildlife to its shores. Keep an eye out for common and grey seals, as well as shore-nesting birds and migrating species.

The area is part of the Blakeney National Nature Reserve and is owned and managed by the National Trust. Access is via boat (normally as part of a seal-watching trip) from Morston or Blakeney, or by foot from Cley next the Sea. Once there you will find a Visitor Centre (a former lifeboat house), open from May to September (opening times can vary depending on tides; check www.nationaltrust.org.uk for details).

The often muddy National Trail runs above the saltmarsh to Blakeney

Continue on the track as it gradually curves round right again to pass a sign giving details of the realigning of the River Glaven that flows out from Cley next the Sea. It was re-routed in 2006 as part of a project by the Environment Agency to help stop flooding to the nearby villages. From this point you will also spot the site of Blakeney Chapel.

BLAKENEY CHAPEL

Although marked as a 'chapel' on the OS Explorer map there is little evidence to suggest that it was used for religious purposes. There have been several archaeological investigations, most recently in 2005, which helped decipher its structure, but looking at it from the vantage point of the Norfolk Coast Path you will see nothing other than a faint depression in the ground to suggest its presence. Indeed it is thought that most of the stone from which this building was constructed – dating from at least 1586 – was reused to build houses in nearby Cley hundreds of years ago.

In 1912 the site was given to the National Trust and what remains is Grade II listed as well as a designated Site of Specific Scientific Interest (SSSI) and one of Natura 2000's Special Protected Areas. As such there is no public access. However, its main threat does not come from man, but from nature. The realignment of the River Glaven has exposed the chapel remains to the effects of coastal erosion. Estimates suggest that if nothing is done to prevent it the site will be buried under the moving shingle ridge in the next 30 years.

Now the path turns a definite right to head south into the village of **Cley next the Sea**. The iconic windmill, rising up above the reeds on Cley Marshes, now dominates the skyline ahead. Follow the path as it brings you closer and closer to the windmill. It may seem tempting at this point to move onto Stage 8 by cutting out the village completely and re-joining the path, which can be seen stretching away to the east – but this is impossible because of the new sluice put in to help realign the River Glaven. Cley is also a worthwhile place to check out (if for nothing else other than to sample the delicious lavender bread in the local delicatessen!). So climb onto the bank in front of you and turn right to follow the (often muddy) path down to the A149.

At the main road turn left, crossing the sluice. Stick to the bank for this, the faster section, of the road, before leaving it via a flight of steps to gain a pavement, which can be followed into the village.

Cley's windmill greets walkers from across the marshes

CLEY NEXT THE SEA

Walking through this idyllic little Norfolk village today, it is hard to picture it as an all-singing, all-dancing harbour town, but it was just that in the 13th century, importing and exporting a range of produce – from wool to coal, grain to fish. Now, far removed from easy access to the sea as a result of the shifting coastline (don't be fooled by its appellation), it is the tourist industry that keeps it afloat. Birdwatching and wedding parties in particular bring visitors flocking in to the marshes and windmill respectively. This iconic structure has long been used as a B&B and honeymoon/wedding venue. There are a number of other accommodation options including self-catering cottages and hotels available. There are several cafés and the aforementioned delicatessen (www.picnicfayre.co.uk) which offers takeaway hot and cold drinks as well as homemade cakes, sandwiches, soups, quiches and pastries.

If you are doing just one stage of the long-distance path there is a free car park at the village hall, signed off the main street, and a Coasthopper stop just outside the delicatessan. For more information about the village see www.cley.org.uk.

STAGE 8

Cley next the Sea to Cromer

Start	Coast Road, Cley next the Sea (TG 044 437)
Finish	The Pier, Cromer (TG 219 423)
Distance	22.5km (14 miles)
Time	6½hrs
Refreshments	Pubs and cafés in Sheringham and Cromer
Toilets	Sheringham and Cromer
Public transport	Coasthopper bus at Cley next the Sea, Sheringham and Cromer
Parking	Public car parks in Cromer
Accommodation	B&Bs, guesthouses and hotels in Cromer

They say that 'nothing worth having in this world comes easy', and whoever 'they' were they must have walked this final leg of the Norfolk Coast Path. Cley Marshes gives way to kilometres of strength-sapping shingle, when the views work hard to compensate for the leg-aching terrain. Once the stones give way to crumbling cliffs the rest is in the bag, from the ever-increasing crowds at Sheringham – where the cliffs rise to a high point – to the final quiet inland jaunt before the Victorian seaside resort of Cromer and journey's end on the pier.

Map continues on page 110

Walking on the shingle beach at Cley next the Sea, heading east

In **Cley next the Sea** the path passes through the village, turning left at the T-junction to follow the main road. At a phone box on your right, and as the road swings right, take the discrete path that cuts down left, parallel to a wall. This emerges into a passageway on the right with a small collection of moorings below left, an apartment block right, and the windmill straight ahead.

Follow the passageway to the quay and cut through the windmill car park where signs direct you through a gate ahead. Pass some cottages that belong to the windmill to the left and continue on a narrow path alongside the reeds to climb up onto the seabank. Walk on above the beach road. ▶

Continue along, passing another reminder of the military past in the form of a gun cupola, as the path bears north towards the sea alongside the orinthologically rich Cley Marshes Nature Reserve.

Purchased in 1926 by the Norfolk Wildlife Trust, **Cley Marshes Nature Reserve** was the first reserve to be established in the UK, and has been so successful that the NWT has used it as a blueprint for

Here you will often spot birdwatchers, who have sighted a rare species from the car, pulling over and getting out their binoculars for a closer look.

other reserves. Marsh harriers, bearded tits, bitterns, wildfowl and waders can all be observed in its reed-rich marshland, which is maintained in perfect condition for resident birds. Since 2007 an eco-friendly visitor centre has offered space for viewing birds as well as exhibitions and interpretation boards on common sightings and how to identify them. The entrance to the reserve is next to the Coasthopper bus stop. For opening hours (which vary between winter and summer), admission fees and special events see www.norfolkwildlifetrust.org.uk/cley.aspx.

Eventually you reach the car park at the sea. From here – if feeling curious – you can walk the approximately 4.5km to Blakeney Point (double that for the round trip) by turning left. The National Trail, however, turns right, following the coast as it works roughly southeast. Now the route is primarily on shingle, which can make for tiring walking. Some people tack this stage onto Stage 7 and end at Weybourne, but with the next 6.5km on this strength-sapping surface it is better tackled when fresh in the morning, rather than as a final hurdle at the end of a longer day.

The path crosses patches of grass and rock initially before petering out to shingle, then rises on to a bank of small rocks. The waymarked path frequently disappears and reappears due to a decision in 2007 to allow the sea to shape the shoreline (prior to this the path was

Geese doing their best impression of a giant bird above Salthouse Marshes

continuously being rebuilt), resulting in a less-than-clear route. But this gives you the option to explore. So pick your way over the shingle, stopping every so often to investigate the abandoned bunkers and gun towers, imagining the coastline and its varied military furniture in years gone by; or, depending on how tired you're feeling (and the state of the tide), walk along the beach. The closer you get to the waves the more solid the ground – but try not to get so distracted by the views of the Weybourne cliffs ahead that you forget to watch out for the incoming tide!

As well as birdwatchers lining the shores, you are likely also to pass a host of fishermen apparently mesmerised by the sea. For the next few kilometres your soundtrack will be the crashing waves – which only just matches the crunching shingle underfoot in volume. ▶

Be warned that it can get really windy along this stretch of the coast.

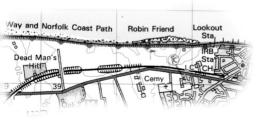

Map continues on page 115

As the cliffs rise above the shingle beach the coast stretches off in the distance all the way to Cromer Pier

Keep a lookout for more birds to the right of the path as you progress along it (on the lagoons of Salthouse Marshes – just after Cley Eye Marshes). At this point you can enjoy two distinctly different views to either side: the verdant green marsh with a smattering of blue pools to the right, the expansive grey of the crashing sea to the left.

Eventually, after what seems like an age (just after the best-preserved bunker, encased by a cloak of shingle) look out for a mast on a small rise to your right, fenced off from the path. This is another remnant of the military past; a whole network of MOD tracks, fences and old buildings stand tall to your right.

For centuries the British coastline has been a weak spot in our defences, and our leaders have strived to create ways to defend us from attack by sea. Although many of the 16th-century batteries and fortifications have been reclaimed by the water, there are still remnants of the **military defences** created in both World Wars in the form of pillboxes, spigot mortar emplacements and gun turrets. Some are starting to show early signs of being lost to the waves too, but there are still extant examples, particularly along the coastline between Weybourne and Cromer, giving a snapshot of what it would have looked like at the height of fear-gripped wartime Britain. At that time the beaches were littered with devices to stop enemy tanks making land, such as minefields and metres of barbed wire. Now, despite these reminders of past battles, a feeling of peace lingers in its place.

Carry on to **Weybourne Hope** where the shingle finally begins to relent as you climb, now on solid ground, onto the cliffs that rise up here at Gramborough Hill. You will pass a crumbling spigot mortar as well as the base of a machine gun device embedded into the cliffs.

The path is a boot-beaten line in the grass. You can stay as close to the cliff edge as you dare, but take heed of the warning about the unstable ground. A careful peer over the edge near some cracks in the cliff will reveal huge swathes that have collapsed onto the beach below.

From here the view becomes truly enticing as the cliffs stretch out onto the horizon and you get a sense that the end is really in sight. At Water Hill the path turns briefly right to pass behind some houses. Once past the buildings turn left through a gate, then left again to walk past the front of them, then right one final time to continue east on the path, the sea once more on your left. At one time the National Trail ran on the seaward side of the houses, but it has been moved inland on account of coastal erosion.

Shortly after passing another bunker (now privately owned) on your right, signs will indicate that you are now on land managed by the National Trust. From here the trail climbs slowly uphill towards Sheringham, passing the many golfers who play on the course to the right. Once again (as with the first part of the Norfolk Coast Path between Hunstanton and Holme) 'watch for flying balls' is the rule of the day. Make your way along the path, at first almost level with the beach, before climbing steeply up Skelding Hill (only 45m above sea level but after the relative flatness thus far it feels like a proper ascent!) to the old coastguard lookout, where the Coastwatch group is based.

> Sheringham is the perfect site for an organisation that keeps a lookout over the Norfolk coast. **Coastwatch** is one of a number of Coastal Surveillance Stations that operates under the charity The Sea and Safety Group UK, keeping an eye on the conditions in the North Sea. The view from the old coastguard lookout (the Watchtower) on Skelding Hill stretches for 22km out to sea. Electricity to the tower is generated via sun and wind power, and walkers on the Peddars Way and Norfolk Coast Path are actively encouraged to stop and wave or say hello (www.sheringhamcoastwatch.org.uk).

Enjoy the views from here both up and down the coast; there is a handy bench where you can stop for a few minutes and reflect on your journey so far. There are still some miles to cover, however, so continue downhill into **Sheringham**, soon entering another townscape.

Feeling solid ground beneath boots as the path leaves the beach at Gramborough Hill

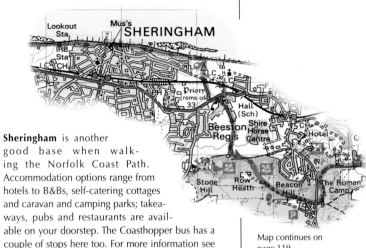

Sheringham is another good base when walking the Norfolk Coast Path. Accommodation options range from hotels to B&Bs, self-catering cottages and caravan and camping parks; takeaways, pubs and restaurants are available on your doorstep. The Coasthopper bus has a couple of stops here too. For more information see www.experiencesheringham.com.

Map continues on page 119

As the sandy path gives way to tarmac, go past the old boating pond and over the toilet block (access via the steps, right, if needed). Continue on and descend the steps on your left to gain the promenade. You will pass a string of cafés and detect the unmistakable aroma of fish and chips as you enjoy the sea-themed paintings on the otherwise bland walls to your right. You will also pass several installations on the Sheringham Art Trail.

Opened in 2008 and completed in 2009, the **Sheringham Art and Sculpture Trail** runs between The Burlington Hotel on The Esplanade (at The Leas) and the seawall paintings at the end of the High Street. It features a mix of paintings, sculptures and murals with a nautical theme that celebrates the local heritage. Part of it can be followed along the National Trail, but if staying longer in the town or using it as a base the trail can provide a colourful diversion (www.open-door-art.com).

Cromer Pier – the end is in sight as you take the final steps along Cromer's promenade

Continue along the promenade and go past the lifeboat house. It is easy to lose sight of the path here, but simply walk along the upper section of the prom to the old toilet block (out of use) and turn right to go up steps, with a steep bank to the left and flats to the right. Follow the concrete path ahead as it slopes up then, at the top, turn left at the putting green. The path is well signposted once again and you follow it up Beeston Hill – a whopping 63m above sea level – marked by an OS trig point. Small it may be, but in a land as low as this those few metres give you truly breathtaking views along the coast. From here you can see the end of the whole 155km (96-mile) route – Cromer – and it looks all too close. But now look inland as that is where you will be headed next as the coast path veers away from the sea one final time.

Follow the steps downhill, heading towards the caravan park. At the bottom an interpretation board gives details of the local wildlife, as the National Trail follows part of the **Beeston Regis Nature Trail** for around one hundred metres. You might spot insects like the white-tailed bumblebee and six spot burnet moth, and birds such as the lesser whitethroat, sand martin and skylark.

Continue straight past this panel. Just as you reach the hedgeline with the caravan park (private property) turn right and follow the path ahead to reach the railway line. Unlike most of the others so far crossed on the National Trail, this train track – the North Norfolk Railway, or Poppy Line – is still operational.

Although only spanning 8km between Sheringham and Holt the **Poppy Line** cuts through the countryside inland, with stops at Weybourne and Kelling Heath in between, both of which offer their own attractions. It was built by William Marriot and operated between 1887 and 1924 when transport by rail was king, then lay unused from its closure until restoration began in 1965. Now it is a very popular tourist attraction, with ongoing work by volunteers undertaken to keep it operational. Both diesel and more traditional steam trains are run, and special events attract hundreds of visitors every year. A museum at Holt gives insight into its past history. For timetables, tickets and opening hours check out www.nnrailway.co.uk.

Take care when crossing the tracks, looking out for any oncoming trains, and follow the path to the A149 once again. Cross over this (watch for fast-moving vehicles) and turn left, passing the sign for the Camping and Caravanning Club, on a minor road that first runs parallel to the main road before branching right. At a T-junction turn right, heading towards Beeston Hall School. Follow the gravel road as it leads slightly uphill bearing south, passing cattle in the fields to your left.

At the top of this road you will see a signpost for the village of West Runton via a bridleway left, but ignore this and take the waymarked National Trail into the trees ahead. It runs parallel to the bridleway at first but then turns to the right once more, gaining a little ascent on a muddy track. Follow it up and out to a minor road and continue straight on between trees. This is adder country, so if you have a dog make sure to put it on a lead.

Identified by the distinct zigzag pattern running down the body and an upside-down V shape on the neck, the **adder** is the only venomous one of Britain's three native snakes. Found mostly in dark wooded areas, they tend not to dart into the undergrowth when they hear someone or something approaching and so are frequently spotted. They are not aggressive creatures (and have not proved fatal to anyone in the UK for over 20 years) but if trodden on or threatened will defend themselves, and so should be observed from a respectful distance.

The stretch of the National Trail where they are most prevalent lies between Sheringham and Cromer, but problems are usually only encountered when a dog sniffs around in their habitat – so dogs should be kept under control. If you (or your canine friend) are bitten remain calm, keep the relevant body part as still as possible (do not restrict the blood flow) and seek immediate medical attention.

Pass a caravan site (right) and a small car park (left). Keep going to pass the highest elevation in Norfolk – **Beacon Hill** at 105m! A short while later you reach Sandy Lane, the minor road that leads down to West Runton. Take care crossing over, and a few steps later take the waymarked track left that leads downhill under trees. All at once it feels very familiar, recalling much of the Peddars Way – yet so close to the finish of the whole route. This is also one of the last places where you may spot a muntjac, so keep your eyes peeled.

The path twists round to the east once more to pass the entrance to a caravan and camping site. Follow it through an avenue of trees; as you cross a small stream and emerge onto Cross Lane look out for the waymarked path on your right. Follow it down a narrow tree-enclosed path, which widens to pass Manor Farm. Head east first to cross the minor road that leads down to **East Runton**, then walk under the giant arched railway bridge that carries the Bittern Line from Cromer towards Norwich.

Head uphill alongside hedged fields but watch out for farm traffic as you go. As the lane levels out you will pass a campsite on both sides, so in summer be wary of cars and campervans coming this way. Follow it as it descends to a road and cross this, bearing right towards the new estate. Suddenly everything feels very suburban as you walk along the pavement between houses. You are now in **Cromer**.

At the main road the National Trail waymarks are still apparent, although they look a little out of place in such a busy and built-up setting. Turn left as signed and follow the pavement downhill. Pass the graveyard, a shopping plaza and the main station.

At the roundabout turn left to walk up Beach Road, now heading north, straight towards the sea; if you listen carefully you may be able to hear the waves as you get closer to the end of the route. Suddenly, as the road begins to descend, the sea is in sight. Cross over the A149; from here you catch your first glimpse of the pier. Turn right and follow the pavement east, passing houses and B&Bs with the promenade below left, to reach a streetlight with fingerposts flaring out just above head height.

This National Trail ends just as simply and understated as it began. The waymarker above your head simply states 'Norfolk Coast Path: Hunstanton 47m', reminding you of the distance you have come. Although this is the official end of the trail, most walkers will continue down the steps to Cromer Pier. There is something

Sunset over Cromer and the coast: a perfect end to a perfect walk

very special about walking out on the Edwardian-style wooden floorboards and heading to the lifeboat station at the end to get a glimpse back at the cliffs stretching into the distance – and that view marks the perfect end to a fantastic walk. All that's left to do is to catch a bus, train or lift home. But as the signpost will kindly inform you, here starts another long-distance walk, so if you still have itchy feet and no commitments… Weavers Way, anyone?

CROMER

Self-proclaimed 'Gem of the Norfolk Coast', this Victorian seaside resort makes a great start or finish point to the entire National Trail. First becoming popular as the result of a good train connection between here and London and the Midlands in the 1890s, tourism still provides its main economy. Accommodation is available in abundance in the form of hotels, B&Bs, guesthouses and self-catering cottages. The Coasthopper bus starts from the bus station, with other bus links to Norwich (and the mainline rail network). Food options are also plentiful, and if you plan to try crab this is the place to do it: Cromer crab has been famous since the 19th century.

There are a number of worthwhile attractions including the lighthouse, the RNLI museum (one of the most decorated lifeboatman Henry Blogg served here: he won the RNLI gold medal three times, the silver medal twice, the George Cross and the British Empire Medal, among others) and the Forest Bed Plantation which contains a wealth of fossils of plants, mammals and ancient manmade tools that date the presence of man in this area to over 700,000 years ago. For more information visit www.thisiscromer.co.uk.

APPENDIX A

Route summary table

Stage	Start	Finish	Distance	Time	Refreshments
1	Car park opposite Blackwater Carr, Knettishall Heath (TL 943 807)	Crossroads in Little Cressingham (TF 873 000)	23.5km (14½ miles)	6½hrs	Thetford, Stonebridge, Great Cressingham (off-route)
2	Crossroads in Little Cressingham (TF 873 000)	Bailey Gate, Castle Acre (TF 817 151)	19km (11¾ miles)	5½hrs	Pickenham, A47, Castle Acre
3	Bailey Gate, Castle Acre (TF 817 151)	B1454, Sedgeford (TF 722 368)	24.25km (15 miles)	6½hrs	Sedgeford
4	B1454, Sedgeford (TF 722 368)	Hunstanton war memorial (TF 672 408)	12.5km (7¾ miles)	3½hrs	Ringstead, Holme next the Sea, Hunstanton
5	Hunstanton war memorial (TF 672 408)	Burnham Deepdale (TF 803 443)	19.25km (12 miles)	5½hrs	Thornham, Brancaster, Burnham Deepdale
6	Burnham Deepdale (TF 803 443)	Stiffkey General Store (TF 969 431)	23km (14¼ miles)	6½hrs	Burnham Overy Staithe, Holkham, Wells-next-the-Sea
7	Stiffkey General Store (TF 969 431)	Coast Road, Cley next the Sea (TG 044 437)	11km (6¾ miles)	3½hrs	Blakeney, Cley next the Sea
8	Coast Road, Cley next the Sea (TG 044 437)	The Pier, Cromer (TG 219 423)	22.5km (14 miles)	6½hrs	Sheringham, Cromer

APPENDIX B
Useful contacts

Websites
The official information source for the Peddars Way and Norfolk Coast Path with all the latest news, an up-to-date accommodation list and contact form to report maintenance issues, request a completer's certificate and buy the official badge.
www.nationaltrail.co.uk/PeddarsWay

English Heritage
www.english-heritage.org.uk

The Long Distance Walkers Association
www.ldwa.org.uk

National Trust
www.nationaltrust.org.uk

Natural England
www.naturalengland.org.uk

Norfolk Wildlife Trust
www.norfolfwildlifetrust.org.uk

Ordnance Survey
www.ordnancesurvey.co.uk

Ramblers Association
www.ramblers.org.uk

Streetmap
www.streetmap.co.uk

Tourist information
www.visitnorfolk.co.uk

Transport operators
National Express
Tel: 08717 818178
www.nationalexpress.com

National Rail
Tel: 0871 200 4950
www.nationalrail.co.uk

Local public transport
www.coasthopper.co.uk
www.norfolk.gov.uk/passengertransport
www.travelineeastanglia.org.uk
Timetables, bus stops and route planners for accessing the National Trail. If you cannot find what you need online call 0871 200 2233.

Tide times/tables
Great Yarmouth Coastguard 01493 851338

Maritime and Coastguard Agency
www.dft.gov.uk/mca
www.tidetimes.org.uk
Tide tables can be obtained from most shops on the Norfolk Coast Path.

Tourist Information Centres
North Norfolk Information Centre
London Road
Cromer
Norfolk NR27 9EF
Tel: 01263 512497
www.visitnorfolk.com

Burnham Deepdale
Deepdale Information (independent)
Main Road
Burnham Deepdale
Norfolk PE31 8DD
Tel: 01485 210256
www.deepdalefarm.co.uk/information

Hunstanton
Town Hall
The Green
Hunstanton
Norfolk PE36 6BQ
Tel: 01485 532610
www.visitnorfolk.com

Sheringham
Station Approach
Sheringham
Norfolk NR26 8RA
Tel: 01263 824329
www.visitnorfolk.com

Thetford
20 Long Street
Thetford
Norfolk IP24 2AP
Tel: 01842 751975
www.explorethetford/co.uk

Wells-next-the-Sea
Staithe Street
Wells-next-the-Sea
Norfolk NR23 1AN
Tel: 01328 710885
www.visitnorfolk.com

Facilities

Peddars Way
Facilities such as public toilets and places to buy food and drink are much harder to find on this section of the National Trail and tend to be at the start and end points of stages, often in hotels and pubs rather than public conveniences. Any additional facilities available en route are mentioned in the relevant stage descriptions, but in general it is best to pick up refreshments for the day ahead at each start point.

Norfolk Coast Path
There are many more facilities on this section of the trail. Nearly every town passed through will have public toilets and in most cases – especially in the bigger resorts – when it comes to food options you will struggle to narrow down your choices rather than desperately seek them out!

LISTING OF CICERONE GUIDES

Mont Blanc Walks
Mountain Adventures in the Maurienne
The Cathar Way
The GR5 Trail
The Robert Louis Stevenson Trail
Tour of the Oisans: The GR54
Tour of the Queyras
Tour of the Vanoise
Trekking in the Vosges and Jura
Vanoise Ski Touring
Walking in Provence
Walking in the Auvergne
Walking in the Cathar Region
Walking in the Cevennes
Walking in the Dordogne
Walking in the Haute Savoie North & South
Walking in the Languedoc
Walking in the Tarentaise and Beaufortain Alps
Walking on Corsica

GERMANY

Germany's Romantic Road
Walking in the Bavarian Alps
Walking in the Harz Mountains
Walking the River Rhine Trail

HIMALAYA

Annapurna
Bhutan
Everest: A Trekker's Guide
Garhwal and Kumaon: A Trekker's and Visitor's Guide
Kangchenjunga: A Trekker's Guide
Langtang with Gosainkund and Helambu: A Trekker's Guide
Manaslu: A Trekker's Guide
The Mount Kailash Trek
Trekking in Ladakh

ICELAND AND GREENLAND

Trekking in Greenland
Walking and Trekking in Iceland

IRELAND

Irish Coastal Walks
The Irish Coast to Coast Walk
The Mountains of Ireland

ITALY

Gran Paradiso
Italy's Sibillini National Park
Shorter Walks in the Dolomites
Through the Italian Alps
Trekking in the Apennines
Trekking in the Dolomites
Via Ferratas of the Italian Dolomites: Vols 1 & 2
Walking in Abruzzo
Walking in Sardinia
Walking in Sicily
Walking in the Central Italian Alps
Walking in the Dolomites
Walking in Tuscany
Walking on the Amalfi Coast
Walking the Italian Lakes

MEDITERRANEAN

Jordan – Walks, Treks, Caves, Climbs and Canyons
The Ala Dag
The High Mountains of Crete
The Mountains of Greece
Treks and Climbs in Wadi Rum, Jordan
Walking in Malta
Western Crete

NORTH AMERICA

British Columbia
The Grand Canyon
The John Muir Trail
The Pacific Crest Trail

SOUTH AMERICA

Aconcagua and the Southern Andes
Torres del Paine

SCANDINAVIA

Walking in Norway

SLOVENIA, CROATIA AND MONTENEGRO

The Julian Alps of Slovenia
The Mountains of Montenegro
Trekking in Slovenia
Walking in Croatia
Walking in the Karavanke

SPAIN AND PORTUGAL

Costa Blanca: West
Mountain Walking in Southern Catalunya
The Mountains of Central Spain
The Northern Caminos
Trekking through Mallorca
Walking in Madeira
Walking in Mallorca
Walking in the Algarve
Walking in the Cordillera Cantabrica
Walking in the Sierra Nevada
Walking on La Gomera and El Hierro
Walking on La Palma
Walking on Tenerife
Walks and Climbs in the Picos de Europa

SWITZERLAND

Alpine Pass Route
Canyoning in the Alps
Central Switzerland
The Bernese Alps
The Swiss Alps
Tour of the Jungfrau Region
Walking in the Valais
Walking in Ticino
Walks in the Engadine

TECHNIQUES

Geocaching in the UK
Indoor Climbing
Lightweight Camping
Map and Compass
Mountain Weather
Moveable Feasts
Outdoor Photography
Polar Exploration
Rock Climbing
Sport Climbing
The Book of the Bivvy
The Hillwalker's Guide to Mountaineering
The Hillwalker's Manual

MINI GUIDES

Avalanche!
Navigating with a GPS
Navigation
Pocket First Aid and Wilderness Medicine
Snow

For full information on all our guides, and to order books and eBooks, visit our website:
www.cicerone.co.uk.

Walking – Trekking – Mountaineering – Climbing – Cycling

Over 40 years, Cicerone have built up an outstanding collection of 300 guides, inspiring all sorts of amazing adventures.

Every guide comes from extensive exploration and research by our expert authors, all with a passion for their subjects. They are frequently praised, endorsed and used by clubs, instructors and outdoor organisations.

All our titles can now be bought as **e-books** and many as iPad and Kindle files and we will continue to make all our guides available for these and many other devices.

Our website shows any **new information** we've received since a book was published. Please do let us know if you find anything has changed, so that we can pass on the latest details. On our **website** you'll also find some great ideas and lots of information, including sample chapters, contents lists, reviews, articles and a photo gallery.

It's easy to keep in touch with what's going on at Cicerone, by getting our monthly **free e-newsletter**, which is full of offers, competitions, up-to-date information and topical articles. You can subscribe on our home page and also follow us on **Facebook** and **Twitter**, as well as our **blog**.

Cicerone – the very best guides for exploring the world.

CICERONE

2 Police Square Milnthorpe Cumbria LA7 7PY
Tel: 015395 62069 info@cicerone.co.uk
www.cicerone.co.uk